STUART MCHARDY is a writer, occasional broadcaster and storyteller. Having been actively involved in many aspects of Scottish culture throughout his adult life – music, poetry, language, history, folklore – he has been resident in Edinburgh for over a quarter of a century. Although he has held some illustrious positions including Director of the Scots Language Resource Centre in Perth and President of the Pictish Arts Society, McHardy is probably proudest of having been a member of the Vigil for a Scottish Parliament. Often to be found in the bookshops, libraries and tea-rooms of Edinburgh, he lives near the city centre with the lovely (and ever-tolerant) Sandra and they have one son, Roderick.

DONALD SMITH is Director of the Scottish Storytelling Centre at Edinburgh's Netherbow and a founder of the National Theatre of Scotland. For many years he was responsible for the programme of the Netherbow Theatre, producing, directing, adapting and writing professional theatre and community dramas, as well as a stream of literature and storytelling events. He has published both poetry and prose and is a founding member of Edinburgh's Guid Crack Club. He also arranges story walks around Arthur's Seat.

Calton Hill

Journeys and Evocations

Stuart McHardy and Donald Smith

Luath Press Limited

EDINBURGH

www.luath.co.uk

First published 2013

ISBN: 978-1-908373-85-4

The publishers acknowledge the support of

towards the publication of this volume.

The paper used in this book is recyclable. It is made from low chlorine pulps
produced in a low energy, low emissions manner from renewable forests.

Printed and bound by
Charlesworth Press, Wakefield

Map by Jim Lewis

Typeset in 10.5 point Sabon by 3btype.com

Contents

Acknowledgements

The authors of this book are grateful to the Scottish Storytelling Forum for its encouragement of this storyguide to Calton Hill, and to the European 'Seeing Stories' landscape narrative project, which is supported by the EU Cultural Programme, funded by the European Commission. We also acknowledge the research of 'Scotland's Cultural Heritage', into the City Observatories presented in *A Caledonian Acropolis* by David Gavine and Laurence Hunter, and the City of Edinburgh Council's exhibition in the Nelson Monument. For those seeking further information about the streets around Calton Hill we recommend Ann Mitchell's excellent book *The People of Calton Hill*. The content of this volume however reflects the views only of the authors, and the information and its use are not the responsibility of the European Commission or any other cited source, but of the authors.

We are delighted that, following the success of our first volume *Arthur's Seat: Journeys and Evocations*, Luath Press is developing a *Journeys and Evocations* series to reach out across Scotland. We look forward to more evocations of our and your special places.

Introduction

Edinburgh's Calton Hill is a volcanic fragment, stubbornly enduring as an untamed space encircled by the city. It was established in 1725 as one of the world's earliest public parks, which was then later populated with a striking – if strange – assortment of monuments. 'Edinburgh,' suggested 20th century bard Hugh MacDiarmid, in a poem of that name, 'is a mad god's dream.' He was surely standing on Calton Hill as he described Leith and the estuary of the Forth 'cleaving to sombre heights'.

But MacDiarmid was only the latest in a long line of poets and philosophers to be gobsmacked by Calton Hill. Lord Cockburn, the Victorian defender of Edinburgh's beauties and inspirer of today's Cockburn Association, was lavish in his eulogy on this exceptional urban landscape. Writing to the Lord Provost of Edinburgh in 1849, he describes Calton Hill as 'the Glory of Edinburgh'.

> 'It presents us,' enthused Cockburn, 'with the finest prospects both of its vicinity and the city… it is adorned by beautiful buildings dedicated to science and to the memory of distinguished men… that sacred mount is destined, I trust, to be still more solemnly adorned by good architecture, worthily applied, so as the walks and the prospects and the facilities of seeing every edifice in proper lights and from proper distances be preserved, and only great names and great events be immortalised; it cannot be crowned by too much high art.'

Today, Edinburgh City Council and the Edinburgh UNESCO World Heritage Trust, which guards Edinburgh's designation as a World Heritage Site, are both labouring admirably to fulfil Cockburn's remit, restoring the diverse monuments and fostering a sense of the Hill as a unified and unique landscape. But they are not wholly in control: Calton

Hill has its own alternative energies. A focus of ancient rituals, modern performances, and political demonstrations, Calton Hill is a public park which is an ungated inner city space: uncultivated and subject to the licence of the night, as well as the enlightenment of the day.

Many artists have been drawn to Calton Hill, as our *Journeys and Evocations* will show, but perhaps pride of place should be accorded to Edinburgh's own Robert Louis Stevenson. Stevenson was a child of the Edinburgh Enlightenment and of its unique concatenation of philosophers, engineers, lawyers and ministers. But what he saw from Calton Hill was a more mixed inheritance of light and dark, mental aspiration mingled with social squalor, moral ideals with human reality. Calton Hill is 'the eye' of Edinburgh through which everything can be seen in nature and in human culture. Even in the Hill's immediate vicinity, the classical order of Waterloo Bridge looks down on the shady chasms of Calton Road below.

Stevenson's famous description of the view from Calton Hill, published in 1889, is our first evocation but towards the end of his life the author, exiled by ill-health to Samoa, returned to Calton Hill in a little noticed story: *The Misadventures of John Nicholson*. The hero is a young man divided like the youthful Stevenson between the respectable Edinburgh world of prosperous terraces (Randolph Crescent in this case) and the dubious twilight of jails and slums that still wrapped itself around the south side of Calton Hill. Clearly, Stevenson is recalling over the decades his own borderland experiences on Edinburgh's Hill of Light.

> He proceeded slowly back along the terrace in a tender glow; and when he came to Greenside Church, he halted in a doubtful mind. Over the crown of the Calton Hill, to his left, lay the way to Colette's, where Alan would soon be looking for his arrival, and where he would now no more have consented to go than he would have wilfully wallowed in a bog...

But right before him was the way home, which pointed only to bed, a place of little ease for one whose fancy was strung to the lyrical pitch, and whose not very ardent heart was just then tumultuously moved. The hill-top, the cool air of the night, the company of the great monuments, the sight of the city under his feet, with its hills and valleys and crossing files of lamps, drew him by all he had of the poetic, and he turned that way; and by that quite innocent reflection, ripened the crop of his venial errors for the sickle of destiny.

On a seat on the hill above Greenside he sat for perhaps half an hour, looking down upon the lamps of Edinburgh, and up at the lamps of heaven. Wonderful were the resolves he formed; beautiful and kindly were the vistas of future life that sped before him... At that juncture the sound of a certain creasing in his greatcoat caught his ear. He put his hand into his pocket, pulled for the envelope that held the money, and sat stupefied... He looked up. There was a man in a very bad hat a little to one side of him, apparently looking at the scenery; from a little on the other side a second nightwalker was drawing very quietly near. Up jumped John. The envelope fell from his hands; he stooped to get it, and at the same moment both men ran in and closed with him.

A little after, he got to his feet very sore and shaken, the poorer by a purse that contained exactly one penny postage-stamp, by a cambric handkerchief, and by the all-important envelope. Here was a young man on whom, at the highest point of loverly exaltation, there had fallen a blow too sharp to be supported alone; and not many hundred yards away his greatest friend was sitting at supper – ay and even expecting him...

Close under Calton Hill there runs a certain narrow avenue, part street, part by-road. The head of it faces the doors of the prison; its tail descends into the sunless slums of the Low Calton. On one hand it is overhung by the crags of the hill, on the other by an old graveyard. Between these two the roadway runs in a trench, sparsely lighted at night, sparsely frequented by day, and bordered, when it has cleared the place of tombs, by dingy and ambiguous houses. One of these was the house of Colette; and at this door our ill-starred John was presently beating for admittance.

So, in Stevenson's recall, Calton Hill and its surroundings embody all the Jekyll and Hyde qualities of Edinburgh. It looks upwards to the starlit heavens while retaining something of Erebean night. Welcome to these journeys into this much-evoked yet little understood glory – 'a mad god's dream'.

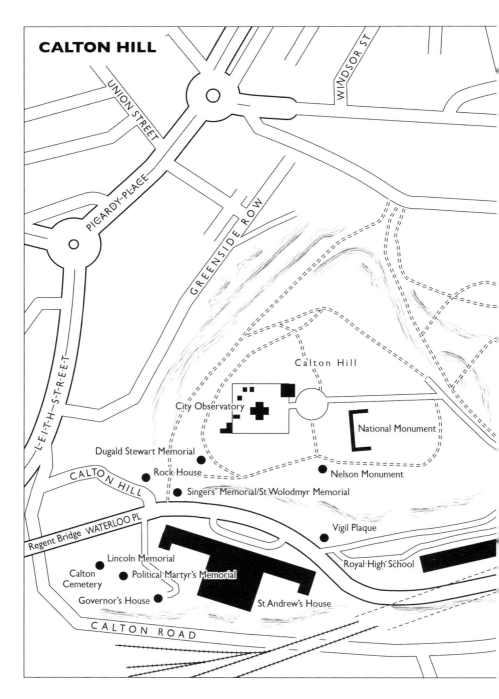

CALTON HILL

UNION STREET

WINDSOR ST

PICARDY PLACE

GREENSIDE ROW

L-E-I-T-H S-T-R-E-E-T

Calton Hill

City Observatory

National Monument

Dugald Stewart Memorial

Rock House

Nelson Monument

CALTON HILL

Singers' Memorial/St Wolodmyr Memorial

Regent Bridge WATERLOO PL

Vigil Plaque

Lincoln Memorial

Royal High School

Calton Cemetery

Political Martyr's Memorial

Governor's House

St Andrew's House

CALTON ROAD

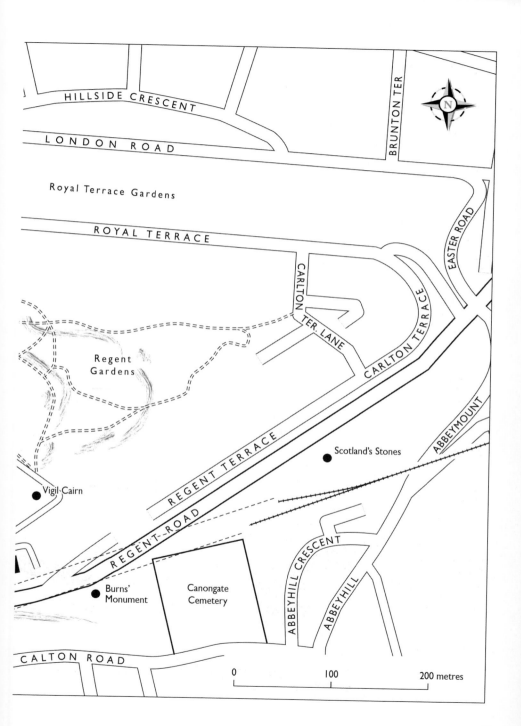

HILLSIDE CRESCENT

LONDON ROAD

BRUNTON TER

Royal Terrace Gardens

ROYAL TERRACE

CARLTON TER. LANE

CARLTON TERRACE

EASTER ROAD

Regent
Gardens

REGENT TERRACE

ABBEYMOUNT

Scotland's Stones

Vigil Cairn

REGENT-ROAD

ABBEYHILL CRESCENT

ABBEYHILL

Burns'
Monument

Canongate
Cemetery

CALTON ROAD

| 0 | 100 | 200 metres |

A Victorian Viewpoint

Robert Louis Stevenson

The east of new Edinburgh is guarded by a craggy hill, of no great elevation, which the town embraces. The old London Road runs on one side of it; while the New Approach, leaving it on the other hand, completes the circuit. You mount by stairs in a cutting of the rock, to find yourself in a field of monuments. Dugald Stewart has the honour of situation and architecture; Robert Burns is memorialised lower down upon a spur; Lord Nelson, as befits a sailor, gives his name to the topgallant of Calton Hill. This latter erection has been differently and, yet, in both cases, aptly compared to a telescope and a butter-churn; comparisons apart, it ranks among the vilest of men's handiworks. But the chief feature is an unfinished range of columns, 'the Modern Ruin' as it has been called – an imposing object from far and near, and giving Edinburgh, even from the sea, that false air of a Modern Athens which has earned for her so many slighting speeches. It was meant to be a National Monument and its present state is a very suitable monument to certain national characteristics. The old Observatory – a quaint brown building on the edge of the steep – and the new Observatory – a classical edifice with a dome – occupy the central portion of the summit. All these are scattered on a green turf, browsed over by some sheep.

The scene suggests reflections on fame and on man's injustice to the dead. You see Dugald Stewart rather more handsomely commemorated than Burns. Immediately below, in the Canongate Churchyard, lies Robert Fergusson, Burns' master in his art, who died insane while yet a stripling and, if Dugald Stewart has been somewhat too boisterously acclaimed as the Edinburgh poet, he is most unrighteously forgotten. The votaries of Burns, a crew too common in all ranks in Scotland and more remarkable for number than discretion, eagerly suppress all mention of the lad who handed to him the poetic impulse and, up to the time when he grew famous, continued to influence him in his manner and the choice of subjects. Burns himself not only acknowledged his debt in a fragment of autobiography, but erected a tomb over the grave in Canongate Churchyard. This was worthy of an artist, but it was done in vain; and although I think I have read nearly all the biographies of Burns, I cannot remember one in which the modesty of nature was not violated, or where Fergusson was not sacrificed to the credit of his follower's originality. There is a kind of gaping admiration that would fain roll Shakespeare and Francis Bacon into one, to have a bigger thing to gape at; and a class of men who cannot edit one author without disparaging all others. They are indeed mistaken if they think to please the great originals – and whoever puts Fergusson right with fame – cannot do better than dedicate his labours to the memory of Burns, who will be the best delighted of the dead.

Of all places for a view, this Calton Hill is perhaps the best, as you can see the Castle, which you lose from the Castle, and Arthur's Seat, which you cannot see from Arthur's Seat. It is the place to stroll on one of those days of sunshine and east wind which are so common in our more than temperate summer. The breeze comes off the sea, with a little of the freshness, and that touch of chill, peculiar to the quarter, which is delightful to certain very ruddy organisations and greatly the reverse to the majority of mankind. It brings with it a faint, floating haze, a cunning decolouriser, although not thick enough to obscure outlines near at hand. But the haze lies more thickly to windward at the far end of Musselburgh Bay and over the Links of Aberlady and Berwick Law and the hump of the Bass Rock it assumes the aspect of a bank of thin sea fog.

Immediately underneath, upon the south, you command the yards of the High School, and the towers and courts of the new Jail – a large place, castellated to the extent of folly, standing by itself on the edge of a steep cliff, and often joyfully hailed by tourists as the Castle. In the one, you may perhaps see female prisoners taking exercise like a string of nuns; in the other, schoolboys running at play and their shadows keeping step with them. From the bottom of the valley, a gigantic chimney rises almost to the level of the eye – a taller and a shapelier edifice than Nelson's Monument. Look a little further, and there is Holyrood Palace, with its Gothic frontal and ruined abbey, and the red sentry pacing smartly to and fro before the door like a mechanical figure in a panorama. By way of an outpost, you can single out the little peak-roofed lodge, over which Rizzio's murderers made their escape and where Queen Mary herself, according to gossip, bathed in white wine to entertain her loveliness. Behind and overhead, lie the Queen's Park, from Muschat's Cairn to Dumbiedykes, St Margaret's Loch, and the long wall of Salisbury Crags; and thence, by knoll and rocky bulwark and precipitous slope, the eye rises to the top of Arthur's Seat, a hill for magnitude, a mountain in virtue of its bold design, upon your left. Upon the right, the roofs and spires of the Old Town climb one above another to where the citadel prints its broad bulk and jagged crown of bastions on the western sky. Perhaps it is now one in the afternoon and at the same instant of time, a ball rises to the summit of Nelson's flagstaff close at hand, and, far away, a puff of smoke followed by a report bursts from the half-moon battery at the Castle. This is the time-gun by which people set their watches, as far as the sea coast or in hill farms upon the Pentlands. To complete the view, the eye enfilades Princes Street, black with traffic, and has a broad look over the valley between the Old and the New Town: here, full of railway trains and stepped over by the high North Bridge upon its many columns, and there, green with trees and gardens.

On the north, the Calton Hill is neither so abrupt in itself nor has it so exceptional an outlook, and yet even here it commands a striking prospect. A gully separates it from the New Town. This is Green side, where witches were burned and tournaments held in former days. Down that almost precipitous bank, Bothwell launched his horse, and so first, as they say, attracted the bright eyes of Mary. It is now tessellated

with sheets and blankets out to dry, and the sound of people beating
carpets is rarely absent. Beyond all this, the suburbs run out to Leith;
Leith camps on the seaside with her forest of masts; Leith roads are full
of ships at anchor; the sun picks out the white pharos upon Inchkeith
Island; the Firth extends on either hand from the Ferry to the May;
the towns of Fifeshire sit, each in its bank of blowing smoke, along
the opposite coast; and the hills enclose the view, except to the farthest
east, where the haze of horizon rests upon the open sea. There lies the
road to Norway: a dear road for Sir Patrick Spens and his Scots Lords;
and yonder smoke on the hither side of Largo Law is Aberdour, from
whence they sailed to seek a queen for Scotland.

> O lang, lang, may the ladies sit,
> Wi' their fans into their hands,
> Or ere they see Sir Patrick Spens
> Come sailing to the land!

The sight of the sea, even from a city, will bring thoughts of storm
and sea disaster. The sailors' wives of Leith and the fisherwomen of
Cockenzie, not sitting languorously with fans but crowding to the
tail of the harbour with a shawl about their ears, may still look vainly
for brave Scotsmen who will return no more, or boats that have gone
on their last fishing. Since Sir Patrick sailed from Aberdour, what a
multitude have gone down in the North Sea! Yonder is Auldhame,
where the London smack went ashore and wreckers cut the rings from
ladies' fingers and a few miles round Fife Ness is the fatal Inchcape, now
a star of guidance; and the lee shore to the east of the Inchcape is that
Forfarshire coast where Mucklebackit sorrowed for his son.

These are the main features of the scene roughly sketched. How they
are all tilted by the inclination of the ground, how each stands out in
delicate relief against the rest, what manifold detail, and play of sun and

shadow, animate and accentuate the picture, is a matter for a person on the spot, and turning swiftly on his heels, to grasp and bind together in one comprehensive look. It is the character of such a prospect, to be full of change and of things moving. The multiplicity embarrasses the eye and the mind, among so much, suffers itself to grow absorbed with single points. You remark a tree in a hedgerow, or follow a cart along a country road. You turn to the city, and see children, dwarfed by distance into pigmies, at play about suburban doorsteps; you have a glimpse upon a thoroughfare where people are densely moving; you note ridge after ridge of chimney-stacks running downhill one behind another, and church spires rising bravely from the sea of roofs. At one of the innumerable windows, you watch a figure moving; on one of the multitude of roofs, you watch clambering chimney-sweeps. The wind takes a run and scatters the smoke; bells are heard, far and near, faint and loud, to tell the hour; or perhaps a bird goes dipping evenly over the housetops, like a gull across the waves. And here you are in the meantime, on this pastoral hillside, among nibbling sheep and looked upon by monumental buildings.

Return thither on some clear, dark, moonless night, with a ring of frost in the air, and only a star or two set sparsely in the vault of heaven; and you will find a sight as stimulating as the hoariest summit of the Alps. The solitude seems perfect: the patient astronomer, flat on his back under the Observatory dome and spying heaven's secrets, is your only neighbour. Yet, from all round you, there come up the dull hum of the city, the tramp of countless people marching out of time, the rattle of carriages and the continuous keen jingle of the tramway bells. An hour or so before, the gas was turned on and lamplighters scoured the city; in every house, from kitchen to attic, the windows kindled and gleamed forth into the dusk. And so now, although the town lies blue and darkling on her hills, innumerable spots of the bright element shine far and near along the pavements and upon the high façades. Moving lights of the railway pass and repass below the stationary lights upon the bridge. Lights burn in the Jail. Lights burn high up in the tall lands and on the Castle turrets, they burn low down in Greenside or along the Park. They run out beyond the other into the dark country. They walk in a procession down to Leith, and shine singly far along Leith Pier. Thus, the plan of the city and her suburbs is mapped out upon the ground of blackness, as when a child pricks a drawing full of pinholes and exposes it before a candle; not the darkest night of winter can conceal her high station and fanciful design. Every evening in the year, she proceeds to illuminate herself in honour of her own beauty and as if to complete the scheme – or rather as if some prodigal Pharaoh were beginning to extend to the adjacent sea and country – half-way over to Fife, there is an outpost of light upon Inchkeith, and far to seaward, yet another on the May.

And while you are looking, across upon the Castle Hill, the drums and bugles begin to recall the scattered garrison, the air thrills with the sound, the bugles sing aloud and the last rising flourish mounts and melts into the darkness like a star: a martial swan-song, fitly rounding in the labours of the day.

Part I:

A Radical Tour

Stuart McHardy

Edinburgh's Princes Street is one of the most famous and dramatic streets in the world. Every year it draws tens of thousands of tourists, who walk along its length thrilled with the great castle looming over it and Arthur's Seat framing the skyline to the east. But looking straight east along the line of the thoroughfare is a smaller hill, less dramatic perhaps than the mighty crag of Arthur's Seat but a significant presence nonetheless. This is Calton Hill, a place with considerable significance in the history of both Edinburgh and Scotland, and the many buildings and structures on it are a reflection of much that is truly dramatic and exciting in the past of this great city.

The oldest name that seems to exist referring to Calton Hill is Craigengalt, which appears in 1589 and did not go out of use till the middle of the 18th century. The name seems to derive from *crag an gallt,* 'the hill of the woods' in Ancient North Brythonic, the language spoken by the local people the Goddodin, who were known by the Romans as the Votadini. This was a language, or dialect, closely related to Old Welsh. The Gododdin disappear from history in the second half of the first millennium but a poem telling of a great raid or battle that they tragically took part in was composed here in Edinburgh around 600AD, and is now accepted as the oldest document in Welsh literature.

It has been suggested that the later form of the hill's name, Calton, means 'the place of the groves', or possibly the 'hill of the hazel trees', as hazels were significant in pre-Christian belief. What these old names underline is the reality that the hill had a place in local society in the far past, though it is intriguing that there have been no truly ancient archaeological finds on the hill. This is perhaps because so much of the hill was built on in the 19th century.

Calton existed as a separate burgh, or town, from Edinburgh even after the 18th century development of the capital had begun. In fact, the

Burgh of Calton retained its own identity and its own officials up to the municipal reforms of 1856, when it officially became part of the City of Edinburgh. For centuries before that, however, the top of the hill appears to have been a burgh commons for the people of Edinburgh.

Today, Waverley Station actually overlays some of the old streets of the Burgh of Calton, and the main street, St Ninian's or Beggars' Row, ran along the line of today's Calton Road and on down to the Port of Leith, passing St Ninian's Chapel above St Margaret's Loch at the side of Arthur's Seat.

In a charter of 1456, King James II – who, like his ancestors and descendants, was King of Scots, not of Scotland – had given the city of Edinburgh the low ground on the north-west side of the hill, now known as Greenside, for the staging of tournaments and other warlike pastimes. This was to try and ensure that the population would be prepared for the next invasion from England, a sad and regular occurrence throughout much of Scotland's often bloody history. However, this being Edinburgh, the area was also used for staging plays, the most famous of which was Sir David Lindsay's *Ane Pleasant Satyre of the Thrie Estaitis,* performed here in 1554. This satirisation of court, church and nobility caused a bit of a stir. It is nice to know that the Edinburgh Festival has such historical antecedents. The play was successfully revived in Edinburgh in 1948 and 1996, and in June 2013 the original six-hour version was performed at Linlithgow Palace.

Situated overlooking the east end of Princes Street, Calton Hill is a striking outcrop scattered with a range of dramatic structures, each of which has its own story. However, given how the city has clustered round the hill, the actual size and shape of Calton Hill itself is no longer too obvious. Today it appears to be bounded by Waterloo Place/Regent Road, the resplendent facades of Regent Terrace and Royal Terrace, the upper stretches of Leith Walk and the steep street running between Leith Street and Regent Road, called Calton Road. However before the construction of the Regent Bridge on Waterloo Place, the hill itself was separated from the rest of Edinburgh by a chasm. Today, Calton Road runs down to Holyrood, below the old Dow Craig, at the foot of this chasm, and the House of the Governor of Calton Jail still stands there alongside the bulk of St Andrew's House. The other side of the hill was effectively marked out by Leith Street, and on the east by the line of London Road. Behind the buildings on Leith Walk lies Greenside, which clearly shows the original boundary of the hill. Truly a hill in the heart of the city, even more so than Arthur's Seat.

When the Regent Bridge on Waterloo Place was built between 1816 and 1819, to connect the thoroughfare of Princes Street via the old Burgh of Calton Hill to the main road south, the line of the new road went through Calton Cemetery. Edinburgh was by then already famous as the home of the Enlightenment and the new way into the heart of the city was seen as matching the magnificence of the New Town, springing up to the north of Princes Street. Traditionally, entry from the south had come in along London Road and up Leith Walk to Princes Street. The bridge itself was designed and built by Robert Stevenson, grandfather of the world-famous novelist Robert Louis Stevenson. Today the remains of the original cemetery lie mainly on the southern side of the road but opposite it there is another smaller remnant of the original burying ground. It is fitting that some of the better known figures of the Enlightenment period are either buried in the Calton Cemetery through which the new road was driven, or commemorated on the hill itself. There is a list of some of the notable individuals buried here on the gate of the cemetery. However the most notable monument was not raised in honour of a philosopher or a scientist, or a poet, but to honour a group of men who have come close to being forgotten in Scotland. Their memorial is not mentioned on the board at the gate.

Towering above the tombs and gravestones, the 90-foot obelisk of grey sandstone was raised in 1840 by public subscription. It is dedicated to the men known as the Scottish Political Martyrs and is a reminder of the ongoing attachment of radical and reforming ideas to Calton Hill itself. These martyrs – Thomas Muir, Maurice Margarot, Thomas Fyshe Palmer, Thomas Skirving and Joseph Gerrald – were sentenced to transportation for sedition to Botany Bay in Australia in 1793. Though they are known as the Scottish Political Martyrs, in fact only Muir and Skirving were Scots. Joseph Gerrald was a West Indian-born English landowner; Maurice Margarot, an English Radical of French descent and Thomas Fyshe Palmer an English Unitarian Clergyman. Thomas Muir was a young lawyer from Bishopbriggs near Glasgow, who already had a reputation as a Radical, and William Skirving was a farmer and a tutor from Liberton in Edinburgh. Their crime? Calling for exactly the same kind of reform of the corrupt political system that the then Prime Minister William Pitt had been demanding in opposition, barely more than a decade earlier.

In the aftermath of the American War of Independence and the French Revolution, the British Establishment was in a state of panic. When the Societies of Friends of the People held a convention in Edinburgh on 12 December 1792, with delegates from across the country and visiting delegates from brother organisations in England and Ireland, a crackdown was inevitable. It was led by Henry Dundas, Secretary of War in the British cabinet, and a man who had absolute control of government in Scotland. He controlled all government finance in Scotland and thus had a stranglehold on patronage. He also hated the radical reformers with a passion.

Muir and the others were arrested and sentenced after what can only be seen as a series of show trials and sentenced to 14 years transportation each. Sentencing Muir, the trial judge Lord Braxfield spoke for the British Establishment when he stated:

> The British constitution is the best that ever was since the creation of the world, and it is not possible to make it better. Yet Mr Muir has gone among the ignorant country people and told them parliamentary reform was absolutely necessary for preserving their liberty.

And this at a time when Parliamentary seats were openly for sale!

At a later trial, that of George Mealmaker, who was charged with sedition for distributing Thomas Paine's book *The Rights of Man*, Mealmaker likened the call for reform to Jesus Christ cleaning the moneylenders out of the temple. Braxfield growled, in Scots, the language he actually spoke, 'Muckle guid it did him, he was hangit tae.' At one point during the trial of Maurice Margarot, the defendant came out of his lodgings at the Black Bull on Leith Street to find that a crowd had gathered and had unhitched the horses from the carriage he was taking up to the High Street where his trial was being held. Some of the gathered crowd took the place of the horses and began to haul Margarot up and onto the North Bridge. This was a common practice of showing support. However, though Margarot may have had the support of many the common people, he did not have the support of Dundas! The buildings at the end of Princes Street were filled with sailors from ships moored in the Forth and as the crowd approached they charged them, bludgeoning many of them to the ground and scattering them. Such popular support for a man accused, and set to be found guilty, of sedition, could not be countenanced.

Thomas Muir, the young lawyer from Huntershill, by Bishopbriggs, did manage to escape from Botany Bay and, after a brush with Native Americans near Vancouver and being held prisoner in the Spanish colony of Mexico, eventually made it to Paris where he was treated as a hero by the Revolutionary government. Sadly by then he had suffered serious facial injuries when the Spanish ship on which he was being sent to Spain was attacked and captured by British naval vessels. This appears to have weakened him considerably, and although early reports of his death in the engagement were wrong, he died in Paris in 1797. Before he died, however, he called on the Revolutionary Government of France to provide him with weapons to sail to Scotland and mount an armed uprising against the British Government. By then his Radicalism had clearly strayed into fantasy but to this day he is known throughout the English-speaking world beyond Britain as a fighter for justice and liberty, and as a great orator. His closing speech at his trial in 1793 has been memorised by generations of American schoolchildren:

> As for me I am careless and indifferent to my fate. I can look danger and I can look death in the face, for I am shielded by the consciousness of my own rectitude. I may be condemned to languish in the recesses of a dungeon, I may be doomed to ascend the scaffold; nothing can deprive me of the recollection of the past – nothing can destroy my inward peace of mind arising from the remembrance of having discharged my duty.

It is sad indictment of the long-term lack of teaching of Scottish history in our schools that he remains so little known in his native land. Thankfully the current government at Holyrood are now taking steps to address the situation.

There have long been rumours that Muir met the poet Robert Burns and there is little doubt that his great paean to Scottish history, *Scots Wha Hae*, was inspired by the Radicals of the time, though whether the two of them did meet is as yet unproven. The Martyrs, apart from Muir and Margarot, all died in the southern hemisphere but such was the attachment to their memory that after the passing of the Reform Bill in 1834 (1832 in England) a public declaration of remembrance attracted lots of support throughout Britain. The Radical MP Joseph Hume started a movement to have a monument erected to them in 1837 and on 21 August 1844, the foundation stone was laid with over 3,000 people in attendance. The monument was designed by Thomas Hamilton who also designed the Royal High School and the Burns Monument further east along Regent Road. Another memorial to them was raised in Nunhead Cemetery, Southwark, London.

When, at last, in 1832, the Reform Bill had passed through the Westminster Parliament, getting rid of the corruption of the buying and selling of Parliamentary seats, and extending the electorate, there was great rejoicing in Edinburgh. Scotland's electorate soared from just 5,000 to 60,000, still far short of universal suffrage but certainly a step in the right direction. A great demonstration of support took place in Holyrood Park, attended by many thousands of people. Two years later when Earl Grey, who had been the most enthusiastic supporter of the Bill in Parliament, came to Edinburgh, a great dinner was held in his honour. Three thousand people attended the event and fittingly, the dinner took place in a great marquee erected on the top of Calton Hill.

The Political Martyrs' Monument is not the only notable memorial here in the cemetery. Apart from the tombs of the renowned philosopher David Hume and the noted publisher William Blackwood, which are mentioned on the board at the gate, and a memorial to Dr Robert Candlish, one of the more prominent figures in the Disruption of the Scottish Church in 1843, there is one that is topped with a striking statue of Abraham Lincoln. This is the memorial to the Scots who fell fighting for the North in the American Civil War and bears the inscription, 'To preserve the jewel of liberty in the framework of Freedom.' As many of those who had subscribed to the raising of the Martyrs' Monument were supporters of the anti-slavery movement. It seems fitting that they are so close to one another.

Another notable person buried here, though his grave is unmarked, is Peter Williamson (1730–1799). His life story is truly remarkable. Nicknamed 'Indian Peter', he was a lad from Huntly in Aberdeenshire, who ran away from home to Aberdeen when he was just 12. Here, he was kidnapped and transported to America. Sold as an indentured servant – a virtual form of slavery – for seven years, he was fortunate in that his new master was a humane man, who had suffered a similar fate himself when he was young. He sent Peter to school and when he died, left him a sum of money in his will when Peter was still just 17. After marrying and beginning to farm a small tract of land, he got caught up in the war between Britain and France in the 1750s and ended up being kidnapped again – this time by Native Americans fighting for the French. They kept him as slave but after a year he managed to effect his escape when, finding that his wife had died, he returned to Scotland. Here he eventually sued the Town Council of Aberdeen who had been complicit in his original kidnapping. His suit was successful and he moved to Edinburgh where he set up the city's first Penny Post service in 1773.

Overlooking the south-east corner of the Cemetery is a striking building, the Governor's House, all that remains of the once notorious Calton Jail. This was initially built in the 1790s and loomed darkly over the Old Town. Its striking position up on the Dow Crag led many first-time visitors to Edinburgh to mistake it for the castle itself. It was a truly inhospitable place and was the site for executions into the 20th century. During the First World War, the jail kept up the Calton Hill's reputation for Radical connections. It had as prisoners some of Scotland's most fervent left-wing agitators.

John MacLean, the famous Glasgow Republican Socialist, had opposed the war from the outset, declaring it to be no more or less than an Imperial War between Britain and Germany. He was very active amongst the Clydeside ship-workers and after the Government pushed through an act in 1915 prohibiting strikes, he was on a direct collision course with them. Rents were being increased but wages were being cut, and many workers found themselves in difficult situations. It had also not skipped their attention that though wages were being controlled, profits were not, and the shipyard owners were doing very well indeed out of the war. On 26 March 1916 the call from the Clyde Workers Committee (CWC) went out for the shipyard workers to strike.

The declared leaders of the CWC were Maclean, James D MacDougall, John Maxton and Willie Gallacher, later to become Britain's only avowedly Communist MP (so far). Another of the leaders, Davie Kirkwood, later to become the Labour peer, Lord Kirkwood, was deported from Glasgow to Edinburgh then locked up in the castle. In April, Maclean, Gallagher, John Maxton and Macdougall were all put on trial for sedition. They were, of course, found guilty and all spent some time in Calton Jail, which according to Gallacher was:

> by far the worst prison in Scotland; cold, silent and repellent. Its discipline was extremely harsh, and the diet atrocious. The one hour's exercise in the morning was the sole opportunity we had of seeing each other, when desperate attempts were made to exchange a whisper or two. For breakfast, we had thick porridge and sour milk. For dinner, soup and a piece of dry bread. And for supper, thick porridge and sour milk.

However, the government soon realised that keeping these men in jail could only create further trouble in the Clyde shipyards and in February 1917 Gallacher, MacDougall and Maxton and John Muir, editor of the publication *The Clyde Worker*, were released. MacLean, who had been moved to Peterhead was kept behind bars for somewhat longer, being released on 30 June after widespread agitation. By now, the Russian Revolution had taken place and Maclean went on to be appointed as the Bolshevik Consul for Scotland in January 1918.

Nowadays all that remains of the prison is the Governor's House which sits directly over Waverley Station and rumour has it that a certain politician has his eye on it as the official residence of Scotland's First Minister after Independence. It would perhaps be a worthwhile gesture to Scotland's Radical past.

Just past the northern segment of the Cemetery, there is a row of 18th century houses on the side of the hill itself, on the eastern side at the top of the steep street called Calton Hill, and something truly revolutionary took place in one of them in the 1840s. This is Rock House, the building nearest to Regent Road, where the painter David Octavius Hill and Robert Adamson joined together to create Scotland's first ever photographic studio. Their role in the history of photography is of paramount importance as they developed the Calotype process of fixing images which is still in use to this day by some photographers and printers. This had been invented in England by William Fox Talbot, a friend of Adamson's brother John, professor of chemistry at St Andrew's University. Encouraged by his brother, Robert came to Edinburgh to set up a studio and met Hill. They began working together and developed the new process which allowed them to make the first true negatives, from which multiple prints could be made. It was an arduous, complicated, and dangerous process because of the chemicals involved. It was fortunate for Hill and Adamson that Edinburgh was going through a remarkable series of summers in the early 1840s, summers in which for weeks on end there was hardly a cloud in the sky during the long Scottish days. This was of fundamental importance as the photographic plates had to be 'fixed' through exposure to sunlight. They have been said to have created 'the first substantial body of self-consciously artistic work using the newly invented medium of photography.'

Hill and Adamson also left a record of their times which included a photographic record of the men involved in the Disruption of 1843, when 450 ministers left the Church of Scotland to found the Free Church, including the above mentioned Robert Candlish. This was of course part of the ongoing commitment to democracy that had so informed the Radicals of the 1790s and those who came after them, as the Disruption was in part created by a resistance to the corrupt patronage that saw the livelihoods of Presbyterian ministers resting in the hands of a class of people whose only notable attribute was that they owned large areas of land. The Reform Bill of 1832 had been brought about by the need to remove such corruption from the process of selection of Members of Parliament in Westminster.

Rock House became the centre of Hill and Adamson's experimental work and they went on to record groundbreaking series of landscape images, and remarkable and vibrant pictures of a range of Scottish people from everyday walks of life. Their pictures of Newhaven fishwives in particular have become particularly well-known, but they photographed many ordinary working people of the time. The importance of this, though not fully appreciated at the time, is difficult to over-estimate, given that they created what are effectively the first visual ethnographic records, laying the basis for so much of what has happened world-wide since. Although they did photograph luminaries like Hugh Miller, author, geologist, and religious reformer, their images of Newhaven fishwives and other Edinburgh residents give us a remarkable sense of Scotland, and its capital in their time. Sadly, the process of making Calotypes involved the use of chemicals whose noxious effects were as yet unappreciated, and this must have aggravated Adamson's already poor health. He died at the age of 27 in 1848, to the great distress of Hill. Hill and Adamson were very much at the cutting edge of modern technology in their own time and their legacy continues to inspire photographers and print-makers in Scotland,

and throughout the world, to this day. The Scottish National Portrait Gallery has an important collection of their work and some of the images they created can truly be said to be iconic.

On Regent Road, at the side of Rock House, there is a set of stairs leading to a walkway round the hill, and a set of steps which lead up towards the observatory. As you go up these stairs on the right hand there is rock face where a couple of plaques have been mounted in the living rock. One is in memory of three well-known Scottish singers of the 19th century. John Wilson (1800–1849), John Templeton (1802–1886), and David Kennedy (1825–1886) had toured the world singing to audiences often made up of emigrant Scots and the Town Council put the plaque up in 1894. Their repertoires were essentially Scottish and it is reflective of contemporary Scottish culture that these men who travelled world singing 'the auld Scots sangs', many by Burns, and Wilson in particular singing Jacobite material, had all started out as precentors singing in church.

Alongside their plague is something totally different. This is a plaque to St Wolodymyr of the Ukraine and shows an image of him wearing a helmet, flanked by an Orthodox cross and an Ukranian symbol, and the dates 988 and1988. The inscription reads, SAINT WOLODYMYR THE GREAT / RULER OF UKRAINE / 1000 YEARS OF / CHRISTIANITY IN UKRAINE / ERECTED BY UKRANIANS IN SCOTLAND. This underlines the fact that Edinburgh is, and has long been a cosmopolitan city, with communities of many different origins happily living here together. This even includes people from Glasgow.

On the other side of Regent Road, directly on the site of the Old Calton Jail, is St Andrew's House. A striking example of Modernist architecture raised in the 1930s, it was referred to by some, in the years before the institution of the Scottish Parliament, as Scotland's Lubyanka. The Lubyanka was, of course, Moscow's famous headquarters of the

notorious security services (KGB) and a prison for political prisoners, and though St Andrew's House has never been anything other than an administrative office block, its predecessor, Calton Jail, did have a role in housing Scottish political prisoners. It is an imposing building, built in a truly grandiose style and some might say perfect for what was in effect a colonial form of governance in Scotland until 1997. Nowadays, it is home to the administration of the Scottish Government and this would no doubt have pleased the likes of the left-wing agitators John Maclean and Willie Gallacher, sometime prisoners in Calton Jail. Most Socialists of the late 18th and 19th century in Scotland were firm proponents of Home Rule. It was a cornerstone of both Labour and Liberal Party policy in the same period. The Scottish Government's Website has a section of recollections from people who worked in St Andrew's House over the years.[1]

Opposite St Andrew's House and just to the left of the road leading up to the hilltop from the entrance gate to the old Royal High School, there is a small brass plaque on the wall. This commemorates a unique event in Scotland's political history that both drew on, and continued the Radical theme. On 10 April 1992, Scotland had voted out the Conservatives while England had voted them in. Thus Scotland, one of the constituent nations of the United Kingdom of Great Britain and Northern Ireland, had no democratic involvement in the governance of the United Kingdom whatsoever. A protest was called for the following weekend and 400 or so people turned up, mainly contacted through the networks of the anti-Poll Tax and anti-nuclear movements. They gathered at the gate of the Old Royal High School, which had been designated as the putative Scottish Parliament in the run up to the Devolution Referendum of 1979. This, of course, had been derailed by the Westminster Government imposing a condition that Devolution

[1] http://www.scotland.gov.uk/About/Locations/St-Andrews-House-1/sah-70/insidestories

would only be 'allowed' if more than 40 per cent of those voting were in favour. By such rules many then MPs, and even more now, would have never been allowed to sit in the Westminster Parliament, where first-past-the-post is the accepted procedure.

This background had not been forgotten by any of the people who gathered to protest on Regent Road that night. There was a definite buzz of excitement in the air and before long the intended weekend protest vigil turned into something else. For the next five years, the Vigil for a Scottish Parliament existed on the pavement there on Regent Road. A brazier was lit to 'keep the flame of freedom burning' and Pat Kane of the Glasgow band 'Hue and Cry' paid for a Portakabin to provide some shelter for the 24-hour presence. It can get very cold on the Regent Road in winter – even in a Portakabin. From the start the Vigil was manned by a hardy group of regulars supplemented by people from all over Scotland – from every kind of political and social background – who arrived to 'put in a shift' of at least two hours. Individuals and groups of supporters would come from as far away as Inverness and the Hebrides, as well as many closer places, to put in time at the Vigil. Though it did evolve, loosely, into the organisation known as Democracy for Scotland, it was always essentially a single-issue group rather than a political party, though various political parties did, unsuccessfully, try to take it over. The people at the Vigil stuck it out till the Labour General Election victory of 1997. Even some lifelong Tories came along and gave financial support.

The Vigil's continued existence was particularly important as the Labour Party's involvement in the initial period after the election result of 1992 was to set up Scotland United and organise groups all across the country. This became the biggest organisation in a series of large demonstrations in various parts of the country, until, with no warning whatsoever, after 18 months, the two gentlemen co-ordinating Scotland

United, who worked for a then Labour MP, both quit on the same day. Scotland United collapsed and one can only assume that this had been foreseen. The MP concerned was one George Galloway, arch-enemy of the Establishment. However, the death of Devolution was not assured.

At the time the media were going through a process of what can only be described as extreme dumbing down, and the Vigil came to play a key role in sustaining political coverage. From the start there had been street events like 'Not the Royal Garden Party', democracy marches all over Scotland and concerts on the top of Calton Hill, but suddenly the role was different. With this dumbing down of the press, in particular, it became almost a hard and fast rule that every story had to have a picture. So, whenever there was any mention of Devolution, newspaper editors in Scotland said, 'Where's the picture?' and a photographer would be sent to the Vigil to get the necessary photo. This is not the only reason Devolution refused to die but it is part of the story. What would Hill and Adamson have thought? The Vigil eventually came to an end when the election results of 1997 were announced, by which time the late Labour leader, John Smith, had committed his party to the institution of a Scottish Parliament. However most of the people who attended the Vigil believed that Labour had tried to destroy the Devolution movement some four years earlier. The old cliché that politics makes strange bedfellows was proved right again.

To keep themselves from being totally bored out of their minds, the people at the Vigil would discuss all sorts of aspects of Scottish culture – there were casual classes where Thomas Muir and John Maclean were the topics, as well as a host of discussions in all sorts of themes, and many impromptu music sessions. Often the Vigil fire was tended by a just a single demonstrator, but it carried on. And the Vigil laid a wreath of white roses at the Martyr's Monument every 12 December.

The very first night of the Vigil people gathered at the gates of the Old Royal High School and moved to the other side of the road the following Monday. Built in the 1820s, the Royal High School had been left empty when its pupils moved to a new building at Barnton in 1968. During the agitation for a devolved Scottish Assembly in the 1970s the building was proposed as the location and was duly refurbished. As has been noted above, the British Government had decreed that the 1979 referendum for a Scottish Parliament had to have at least 40 per cent of the total electorate voting in favour. This was not achieved so the Assembly was not introduced leaving the newly refurbished Royal High School as a reminder of what might have been. No other vote in the history of British government has ever had such a limitation imposed on it. It is enough to make you think that the British Establishment was anti-democratic.

There are also many people who think that the Royal High School would have sufficed for the Scottish Parliament instead of spending hundreds of millions of pounds on the somewhat eccentric building that now houses that institution opposite the Royal Palace of Holyrood, ironically almost exactly on the site of the old Debtor's Prison of Edinburgh. Rumours that the builders of the new Parliament referred to it as 'The Wee House in the Puddle', due to there being some uncapped wells below its foundations will hopefully not prove to be prophetic. As the century came to a close mutterings were heard around the Capital that the old Royal High School building was far too much of a 'nationalist icon' for it to be the site of the new Parliament. Better to spend all that money than encourage the Nats. Such is politics.

Almost opposite the old Royal High School on the other side of Regent Road there is another neo-Classical structure also designed by Thomas Hamilton. This is the monument to Robert Burns, one of the world's greatest ever poets. His works have been translated into hundreds of languages and his place at the centre of Scottish culture is unassailable. It is, of course, of some interest that he was himself sympathetic to the Radical agitation of the 1790s and a man whose commitment to democracy and equality was unsurpassed. His great international anthem 'A Man's A Man' may have arisen out of him reading the works of the Radical political philosopher Thomas Paine and to this day it is a stirring work in its call for equality and brotherhood amongst all humans.

> Then let us pray that come it may
> As come it will for aw that
> That man tae man the world ower
> Shall brithers be for aw that.

Burns spent some time in Edinburgh and his long-term correspondent and perhaps muse, Mrs Agnes McLehose, whom he called Clarinda, lived just along the road at 14 Calton Hill. Another of his Edinburgh friends, and drinking partner, Willie Nicoll, for whom he penned the song, 'Willie Brewed a Peck o Maut', lies in an unmarked grave in Calton Cemetery.

The monument to Scotland's National Bard had a chequered beginning. In 1812 in Bombay a suggestion was put forward by one John Mitchell that a statue of Burns should be erected on Calton Hill. It wasn't till 1819 that things progressed, however, and the sculptor John Flaxman was hired to create a white marble statue of the poet, based on the portrait by Alexander Nasmyth. Such was the popularity of Burns that the funds raised for the statue – unlike those for the replica Parthenon on the top of the hill – were more than twice the cost of the statue so the Monument was built to house it. The building was finished in 1831 but only a few years later the statue had to be moved because smoke from the gasworks down below it on Calton Road threatened to stain it. Nowadays it can be seen in the Scottish National Portrait Gallery

on Queen Street, not far off. The monument overlooks the Canongate Cemetery which is on the lower slopes of Calton Hill and in which Clarinda is buried.

It does perhaps say something about the people of Edinburgh, or certainly their political representatives, that the monument to the unsurpassable Bard is almost hidden out of the way, along Regent Road while the (much larger) monument to Sir Walter Scott, a true British Establishment figure if there ever was one, towers over the east end of Princes Street. That said, Walter Scott may have contributed greatly to the unfortunate tartan and shortbread image of Scotland which so many Scots resent today, but he also cared deeply about Scottish history and helped keep it alive through his various writings. It seems fitting given the radical and nationalist image of Calton Hill that the Burns Monument sits here, overlooking the Canongate Cemetery.

Above the Canongate Cemetery at the side of Regent Road, with a grand view of the Old Town and Arthur's Seat is the 'Stones of Scotland'. This is a circle of 32 rocks and slabs, one each for Scotland's local authority areas, created by the late, and truly great, sculptor George Wyllie. He was partly inspired by a line by the poet Hugh MacDiarmaid which referred to 'a statue carved out in a whole country's marble'. It commemorates the rebirth of the Scottish Parliament and was finished in 2002. In an echo of ancient Scottish chiefly (and possibly royal) inaugurations, there is a footprint carved in the central stone and George was quoted in the Scotsman as saying:

> This is a stone soap box; Stones of Scotland is like a mini-parliament. People can come along and put their foot in stone and make a wee speech – the ordinary guy saying what he thinks about the parliament.

This wasn't the first time Wyllie had contributed work to Calton Hill. In 1993 he donated a wooden cannon – placed as if firing on St Andrew's House – to the Vigil for a Scottish Parliament and his 1985 Edinburgh Fringe mobile sculpture event, 'The March of the Standing Stones', had included Calton Hill amongst its venues. Humour was always a strong component of Wylie's work and the idea of a wooden cannon pointing at St Andrew's House underlined the absolute commitment to peaceful protest that the Devolution cause, and the Independence movement, in Scotland have espoused.

Above Regent Road on the side of the hill running to the east into Carlton Terrace and round to Royal Terrace is a façade of extremely grand houses. These were designed by William Playfair with the gardens behind the houses designed with the assistance of the botanist Patrick Neill and Dr Robert Graham, Regius Keeper of the Royal Botanic Garden and Professor of Medicine and Botany. This development removed a considerable amount of the common land of Edinburgh, passing it into private, wealthy, hands, with the absolute acquiescence of those representatives of the people themselves, the Council.

While Regent Terrace is still virtually all private homes, several of the town houses on Royal Terrace have been converted into upmarket hotels, one of which has a reputation for ghostly visitations of various kinds. The views over the Forth from Royal Terrace are truly breathtaking. Over the years since it was built a succession of famous people have lived here including the painters Sir George Harvey – one of the founders of the Royal Scottish Academy – and Francis Cadell, one of the leading Scottish Colourists. Various high-level civil servants and other so-called dignitaries have also lived here as well as a succession of expatriate French aristocrats. On the wall of number 28 Regent Terrace is a brass plaque commemorating its role as the Scottish Free French House in the Second World War. On the plaque are these words

'*L'Alliance Franco Ecossaise, La plus vielle alliance du monde.*'
The Franco-Scottish Alliance, the oldest alliance in the world.
This reflects the reality that for centuries Scotland and France were
members of The Auld Alliance, from 1295 to 1560, united in opposition
to the expansionist policies of England. At the far end of Royal Terrace
just inside the entrance to the hill itself behind Greenside Parish Church
there is a small path, hardly used today, which goes down to Greenside,
a quiet and hidden part of the city. Going down it and up onto Leith
Walk there is no hint now that this was once a place of considerable
importance in the social and artistic activity of Edinburgh.

Ascending to the hilltop, the most striking monument on Calton Hill
is the unfinished replica of the Parthenon in Athens. It is in keeping
with the Classical tone of so much of the surrounding architecture,
including the Observatory, the Dugald Stewart and Burns Monuments,
and the Royal High School. But what is most striking about it is the
fact that it is clearly unfinished. Originally it was planned as a full
replica of the Parthenon, incorporating a large church, but only the
front pillars and small parts of the sides were created. A plan for an
equestrian statue of George IV at one corner was also mooted but
dropped.

The original intention for what appears to be no more than a 19th
century folly, was for a memorial to all those Scottish soldiers who had
died fighting abroad in the Napoleonic Wars. It was well-established
practice by the beginning of the 19th century for Scottish regiments to
be the front-line troops in the brutal expansion of the British Empire
throughout the world, and when war broke out yet again with the
Old Enemy, France, Scots were again at the forefront of many battles.
Though France was England's Old Enemy, as we have seen, Scotland
and France had been part of The Auld Alliance which had run from
1295 till 1560 when the Treaty of Edinburgh was signed paving the

way eventually for James vi, King of Scots to become James i of Great Britain in 1603, on the death of Elizabeth i, of England.

Although many people have maintained that the Calton Hill monument was to be raised in commemoration of the fallen, a document of the time expresses the true idea behind the monument rather more clearly:

> At the conclusion of the late war, it was in contemplation to raise a splendid edifice in the Metropolis or its vicinity, as a National Monument, in commemoration of the Naval and Military Achievements of the British Arms.[2]

The British Government was sure that the idea of creating such a conspicuous memorial on Calton Hill would be popular in Scotland so the monies required were to be raised by public subscription starting in 1823. Yet again the design was created by Playfair, though this time with the help of Charles Cockerell. It was intended, once the building was raised, to create a series of catacombs where notable and important public figures could be buried. It was to be, among its other functions, a prominent Mausoleum looking out over the city. The target figure was £42,000 and prominent Edinburgh citizens like Sir Walter Scott and Lords Cockburn, Elgin and Jeffrey pushed the project hard. Yet, for some reason, the people of Scotland seemed reluctant to commit and by the time building commenced only £16,000 had been gathered in. The King himself, George iv, had laid the foundation stone in 1822, with a great display of pomp, including, as well as a considerable Regimental presence, members of the City Council and a parade of Masonic lodges.

But there were not enough Scots keen to give their pennies to such a blatantly Imperialist folly and the over-confidence shown when the

---

[2] N Cleghorn, G 1824. Remarks on the Intended Restoration of the Parthenon of Athens as the National Monument of Scotland

20

building was started in 1826 became all too clear when funds ran out three years later. Perhaps what had happened to Muir and his friends a couple of decades earlier had not been forgotten. Of course, many commentators thought this in shockingly bad taste and it was dubbed 'Edinburgh's Disgrace' by those who were shocked at the Scots' reluctance to back such an important 'national' project.

Over the years there have been various projects mooted to develop it further – one, in 1907, being that it should be finished as a monument to the Treaty of Union of 1707, but that did not come to pass. However, its use in various Devolution and independence rallies, and in the resurgent Beltane ceremonies, show that it does have a use in modern Scotland. And it is fitting that in a locale with such a communal history that so many of the recent activities have been essentially popular, and even occasionally spontaneous. It is also a constant reminder that the simplistic notions of a truly United Kingdom are not as well-rooted north of the Border as some would have us think.

Further down the hill, just by where the road comes up from Regent Road, is a much more modest monument. This is a simple cairn, built to commemorate all those who took part on the Vigil for a Scottish Parliament outside the gates of the Old Royal High School. It has various plaques and stones from different places built into it and is topped with a fire basket, created by the Govan organisation Gal-Gael. The cairn was raised in 1993 when marchers from the four cardinal directions reached the Vigil having set off from the farthest away points on the Scottish mainland. When the City Council was approached about raising the cairn, the then leader of the Labour Party in Edinburgh (now an MP at Wesminster) Mark Lazarowicz, said, refreshingly, 'no problem, after all, it is the people's hill.' This is particularly relevant when we remember that the Edinburgh mob – the only way the city's inhabitants could make their political opinions known to the so-called leaders of the city in the 17th and 18th centuries was by rioting – tended to turn up on Calton Hill with barrels of beer and bottles of whisky after their exertions.

The use of hill tops for celebrations seems as well-rooted in Scottish culture as their use for more ritualistic reasons. The links with communal activities and Radicalism run deep here. However, as we have seen, there are limits on the idea of Calton Hill being the people's hill. A considerable area of the hill, 12 acres of it, are walled in and known as Regent Gardens. This remarkable piece of real estate is 'communally' owned by the affluent people who own the town houses along Regent and Royal Terraces. Their generosity is such, however, that they will allow access to the gardens for those prepared to pay £240 a year for the privilege. Not something the Edinburgh mob would have been happy to accept, I would think.

From the top of Calton Hill on a clear day the view can be amazing. In winter, when there is snow on the mountains, you can regularly see Schiehallion, over 70 miles to the north, and east of it over the far-off Sidlaw Hills on the far side of the River Tay. The massif of Lochnagar, over 60 miles away can also sometimes be seen. However back in the 18th century, long before even the idea of light pollution, the hill was seen as the natural place for an observatory. Given that the traditional name of Edinburgh was 'Auld Reekie', due partially to the pall of smoke that hung over the high tenements of the Old Town, one can only hope that the winds kept the mirk and smog from the tenements of the Old Town away from the telescopes.

Mostly when people think about the Enlightenment in Edinburgh they remember the philosophical developments of this notable period in the city's history but it was also a time of great scientific advancement. The university had been teaching some level of astronomical studies since the late 16th century and as early as 1736 a university observatory was planned. Due to various political happenings – the Porteous Riots of 1736 and the Jacobite Rebellion of 1745, and its bloody aftermath in particular – nothing much was done until the 1770s. The first observatory was designed by James Craig, the architect behind the design of the New Town. The only remaining part of Craig's original design is Observatory House, a striking building that overlooks the hill, and can nowadays be hired as a holiday home.

The first telescope had a focal length of 3.7m and was pretty much at the cutting edge of technology. Sadly the first observatory only lasted till 1807 but just over ten years later the new building designed by William Playfair was started. In 1822 the new building was designated as the Royal Observatory following the now notorious visit of George IV to Edinburgh which was stage-managed by Sir Walter Scott. Although money was tight over the next few years, things began to improve and by 1834 the site was under the control of Thomas Henderson who was Regius Professor of Astronomy at Edinburgh University and the official Astronomer Royal for Scotland. He was succeeded in this position by Charles Piazzi Smyth. He carried on much of Henderson's work but funding difficulties continued. In 1852, it was Smyth who instituted the system of raising the white ball on the mast on top of Nelson's Tower at 1pm daily to give ships out in the Forth a regular time marker. This actually preceded the institution of the now world-famous one o'clock gun fired at the Castle every day by eight years.

Smyth himself was a fine example of the wide-ranging interests of many 19th century scientists and devoted a great deal of time to studying the Great Pyramid at Giza in Egypt. He went to Egypt and made detailed measurements of every aspect of the Great Pyramid and in 1864 he published *Our Inheritance in the Great Pyramid*. He later expanded this and retitled it as *The Great Pyramid: Its Secrets and Mysteries Revealed*.

Today, his idea that the building was erected using a divinely ordained unit of measurement and linking its construction to ancient Hebrew prophecies continues to find favour amongst those people who are obsessed by the supposed significance of the Pyramids and gematria, the 'science' of holy numbers, but such essentially mystical interpretations did not do his reputation much good amongst his scientific peers, and he resigned as Astronomer Royal in 1888. Even in the 19th century the hold religion had on all aspects of scientific and philosophical thinking may seem surprising but we should not forget that there are still fervent advocates of 'Creationism' attempting to foist their own vision of the world on our children.

As the 19th century drew to an end, the Calton Hill site was pretty much out-dated and astronomers were increasingly using high mountain top sites throughout the world for their observations, a practice in which Piazzi Smyth had led the way. In 1896, the Official Royal Observatory of Edinburgh was moved to the new buildings on Blackford Hill, but some observation work was carried out on Calton Hill until 2009. The location has an honourable place in the history of the development of modern astronomy emphasising that Calton Hill has an importance that stretches well beyond the bounds of Edinburgh.

Another striking monument is the one to Dugald Stewart which sits between the observatory and Rock House. This too was designed by Playfair and is modelled on the original monument of Lysicrates in Athens, as was the Burns Monument, reflecting the central importance of Classical Civilisation in western thought. Nowadays we are beginning to understand, particularly in the light of such archaeological discoveries as those at Ness of Brodgar in Orkney, that the idea of 'civilisation' coming north from Greece and Rome to drag our barbarian ancestors out of their intellectual darkness is a simplistic and essentially erroneous view of the world, but during the Enlightenment this was an article of faith. However, if you believe that the development of cities and literature are the most fundamentally important human steps of all time, you may beg to differ.

Dugald Stewart was an important Enlightenment figure – as Professor of Moral Philosophy from 1785, having already been Professor of Mathematics from the age of 19. He was a local man with strong Ayrshire connections, and his father had been Mathematics Professor before him, so he was steeped in the city's social and intellectual atmosphere. Like many others of his time he was deeply interested in politics. Attracted by the philosophical developments in France he went to Paris in 1788 and 1789, finding himself in sympathy with many of the ideals, if not the practices, of the Revolutionaries there. Such opinions made him somewhat suspicious in the eyes of Establishment figures like Henry Dundas who held the governance of Scotland in a death-grip of corruption and repression at the time.

As the new century opened, Stewart went so far as to give classes in what was then known as political economy, which given how Muir and the other martyrs had been treated less than a decade earlier, speaks of considerable courage. A true polymath, Stewart made a substantial contribution to the intellectual climate of his time, through his lectures and his writings. Students flocked to him and not just from Scotland, but from England, Europe and America. Many of his students went on to great things themselves, one such being Henry or Lord Cockburn who went on to become Solicitor General for Scotland between 1830 and 1834, who wrote:

> To me Stewart's lectures were like the opening of the heavens. I felt that I had a soul. Dugald Stewart was one of the greatest didactic orators.

His lectures on the topic were instrumental in the development of political economy as an academic topic and his work on mathematics, like his philosophical thinking, was of great importance particularly in America and France. Stewart's ideas on linguistic theory have been seen as a turning point in the history of the subject. Such was his prestige that when he died he was seen as 'the pride and ornament of Scotland' and there is no doubt that he was one of the most important contributors to what became known as the Scottish Enlightenment. The monument was raised on Calton Hill after his death in 1828.

Above all the other structures on the hill is the Nelson Monument. It sits in the highest point of the hill (171m/561ft) adding another 32m/105 ft. It was built between 1807 and 1815 to commemorate Admiral Nelson's death at the victorious Battle of Trafalgar in 1805. The tower was funded by public subscription. In a forewarning of what was to come with the finding for the Parthenon replica, the original design had to be rejected as too expensive, and a simpler design was used. Even then it had some funding problems before being finally completed in 1816 when the extended pentagonal ground floor was added. The tower replaced an earlier mast that had long been used to signal ships in the Forth estuary, and the time ball was part of its structure form the beginning. The ground floor was a tea-room for a while in the 19th century before becoming the residence of the tower's caretaker. Public access to the top of the tower was subject to a small charge and the tower was recently renovated. The view over the city and the Forth estuary from the top is spectacular on clear days.

We have seen that Calton Hill is in itself almost a historical document with its references to so many important events and periods in Scotland's past. The history of the Hill is strongly associated with the community of the city of Edinburgh, radical politics and latterly the longing for a return to the independent nation-state of Scotland, betrayed in 1707. For centuries the people of Edinburgh, with no say in the running of the city would occasionally riot to show their displeasure, or express their political views.

There were major riots at the passing of the Act of Union in 1707 and almost 30 years later the famous Porteous Riot saw the Commander of the Town Guard being hanged by the mob, in an event which may have had some Jacobite tendencies, but certainly was partially caused by resentment against government excisemen. Porteous had ordered the Town Guard to fire on people protesting against the hanging of a smuggler Andrew Wilson who had robbed a custom house in Fife. Six people were killed, many more wounded, and though brought to trial, Porteous was set free. At which point the people rose and hanged him.

In June 1792, there was a major riot on the occasion of the King's Birthday and one of the men brought to trial was defended by Thomas Muir, himself about to become much better known. The 1812 New Year's Day riot saw the tradition continue into the new century, even if this one seemed to have led to widespread criminality. What was common to all of these 'activities' was that after the rioting was over, the windows broken, effigies set alight, and battles finished with dragoons and other soldiers, the mob would always head off to the same place. This was of course Calton Hill, overlooking the Canongate and the rest of the Old Town, and here the populace would celebrate by lighting fires, drinking, dancing and singing, before dispersing back to their closes and vennels in the Old Town.

Calton Hill has long held a place in the hearts of the people of Edinburgh. Physically it has many reminders of the intellectual vigour and political commitment of so many individuals who have flourished here in the capital of Scotland. It is almost as if it is a living museum of such aspects of our culture and history. Its physical location looking out beyond Fife to the north shores of the Tay and the Grampian mountains, or over to Ben Ledi, Ben Lomond and Ben Ime to the west, or far to the north to Schiehallion, the Fairy Mountain of the ancient Caledonians, is like a gateway to Scotland itself. Most of these mountains, like the Paps of Fife and North Berwick Law which can be seen much closer, are linked through story, archaeology and place-names to truly ancient rituals and belief. From this small hill in the heart of the capital city, only 338 feet (103m) high, a fascinating spread of Scotland's landscape can be seen, reminding us that even in the heart of a modern Edinburgh we are in the midst of the deep traditions and vibrant history of this ancient country.

Mention has been made of the old links with the French and throughout France there are many statues, paintings and other representation of Marianne, a female personification and national emblem of the country as a whole, who is generally understood as representing Liberty and Reason. The history of Calton Hill and its ongoing associations with the community of the city of Edinburgh suggest that there could be something of a similar spirit inhabiting the ether around Calton Hill. The central figure of the re-established Beltane ceremonies, the Goddess, may in herself reflect this potentiality of the place, while harking back to truly ancient times, when the people of the land saw the ultimate power as residing in female form.

Calton Hill is also important in the aspirations of so many Scots for a fairer and more egalitarian society, which is well understood if generally ignored by the mainstream media, mired as they are in the obsessions of the metrovincial elite in far-off London. The spirit of Calton Hill touches many and sitting as the Hill does, in the very heart of a modern cosmopolitan and ever more confident city, it may, indeed, be seen as a physical reflection of that spirit which informs so much of what makes Scotland what she is today.

Part 2:

Pillars of Folly and Wisdom

Donald Smith

Only a jaundiced eye, or one dulled by over familiarity, can fail to be surprised by the buildings on Edinburgh's Calton Hill. From the unfinished 'Parthenon', to the upturned telescope of Nelson's Monument and the classical purity of Dugald Stewart's memorial, there is an apparent clash of style and purpose which puzzles the inquiring onlooker.

Yet, at the same time, each element in this fantastic conglomeration seems to belong, and the underlying effect is of a unified arrangement, whether arrived at by nature's cunning, chance or human design.

In truth, most of the buildings belong to a period of 50 years from 1780 to 1830, while many of the later constructions are influenced by this period. It was a Promethean age of ambition and folly, linking the 18th century Enlightenment to revolution, industrialisation, war and empire. Over these decades philosophy, science, art, and politics envisaged a humanity set free to achieve its full potential. Old restraints of conventional morality, restrictive creeds and outdated technology are cast aside. Humanity is refashioning its own destiny – or so the myth would have it. The history is more complex and in social terms more mixed, but we cannot take away from that impulse of revolutionary hope and expanding horizons.

For good and ill, what we see on Calton Hill is a Promethean epic, and we must encounter it with the expanding mindsets of our recent ancestors. At the same time, however, we are more aware of ambiguous legacies, of the destructive effects of industrialisation and empire, and of the feet of clay. Our Scottishness is more sceptical and inclined to undercut inflated ambitions. That is fair enough but not if it blinds us to what is actually there. Let's look with fresh eyes and see the stories of the people who inspired these monuments with unclouded vision. Whatever our final judgements, we should expect to be surprised. The hill demands that of us at the very least.

David Hume – Philosophy's Pillar

The Scottish Enlightenment boasts several giants of philosophy, including Adam Smith, Thomas Reid and Adam Fergusson. But the personality who still broods over Edinburgh, and possibly the outstanding philosopher of the 18th century, is David Hume who was born in 1711.

Hume's cylindrical monument in the Old Calton Burial Ground is an ordered tribute to restraint and good taste, but is not quite as disinterested as it first appears. In his time, Hume's reputation in the capital of Presbyterianism was mixed to say the least. He, therefore, took the precaution of funding his own memorial and having it designed by Robert Adam, the leading classical architect of his age. What did he expect from his fellow citizens? Not much, and Hume appears to have judged rightly, since on the night after his burial an armed guard had to be mounted to prevent any desecration of his tomb. Even today the David Hume statue in the High Street, depicting a slightly corpulent Hume in a surrealistic toga and bare feet, attracts a lot of toe rubbers, in search of some irrational contact.

What was the problem? Hume, it was alleged, had questioned the truths of Christianity, making him an atheist, and a heathen atheist to boot, since he was fond of a drink, playing at cards – even on the Sabbath day – and of convivial female company. He had moreover been an enthusiastic supporter of attempts to revive the theatre in Edinburgh, which as the pious well knew was a ploy of the devil.

In one popular tale, the portly philosopher was trudging through the Nor' Loch bog on a short cut from his Old Town lodgings in James Court to inspect the work at his fine newly commissioned residence off St Andrews Square. But he slipped from the path and got stuck up to

his generous waist. Along came a fishwife on the reverse journey and he appealed to her for assistance of the 'help me out, my good woman' variety. 'Aye,' says she, 'you'll be Davie Hume, the atheist. I'll no pou you oot till ye gie me your creed and the Lord's Prayer.' Having been brought up a strict Presbyterian, Hume had the shorter catechism and the Lord's Prayer at his command, and was duly hauled out to proceed on his way. Some later insinuated that the street in which his fine new house was sited had been named 'St David Street' in ironic tribute to the atheist philosopher.

It is not by any means certain that David Hume was an atheist, and he writes about religion with great insight. But he was sceptical about all claims to certain knowledge in whatever branch of human endeavour, and demolished many of them with persistent candour. He did not believe in absolute certainty of any kind, famously arguing that even the common sense information gleaned from sense experience could not be relied upon. There is no guarantee for Hume that the stone you drop in a pool for the hundredth time will sink to the bottom just because this has happened the previous 99 times.

This scepticism challenged scientists and philosophers alike, and Thomas Reid, Hume's successor as the leading thinker of the Scottish Enlightenment, devoted a lifetime to saving experimental knowledge from Hume's critique, so founding the 'common sense' school of thought. This came in time to be called the 'Scotch philosophy'. But the response of such intellectual heavyweights was genteel compared to the fury of religious luminaries who believed themselves to be in possession of divine or revealed truth.

Hume's sceptical cast of thought, and his disaffection from organised religion cost him the Chair of Moral Philosophy at Edinburgh University, and a lifelong deluge of prejudice and misunderstanding, but he remained genial and tolerant throughout. Nonetheless, he left it to his close friend and literary executor, Adam Smith, to publish his dialogues on religion after his death. There is a limit to how much righteous indignation can be borne in one lifetime.

There is much more, however, to David Hume than scepticism of whatever variety. By turning away from preset categories of thought Hume turned the spotlight on the rich complexities of our own experience – the source for Hume of all our ways of seeing and knowing. He was curious about our moral experience, about art and literature, and above all about history, which becomes in his hands an arena of human experiment, the theatre of the passions.

Far removed from the stereotype of cold rationalism, Hume is a consummate prose stylist and a connoisseur of the emotions. His monumental *History of England* was a bestseller and, along with his essays, made him a prosperous man of letters. 'Reason,' he declares, 'is and ought to be only the slave of the passions and can never pretend to any other office than to serve and obey them'. So, while Hume practiced the Enlightenment's 'science of human nature', he believed that all science derives from our human nature with its frailties and contradictions.

Hume himself was not a political revolutionary or socially radical. He would have regarded the claim to 'liberty, equality and fraternity' as an innate human right with characteristic scepticism. His recognition of the power of the human passions in history made him wary of sweeping claims, while cautiously progressive. He might have been a little piqued at being dwarfed in the Old Calton Burial Ground by the towering 'Cleopatra's needle' of the Martyrs Monument, raised to the radical 'martyrs' of the 1790s. The word 'martyr' might not have gone down well!

The Hume inheritance runs through literature, history, psychology and art as well as what might be considered today the more technical discipline of logical philosophy. In this way, Dugald Stewart, the other philosopher commemorated with a classical monument on Calton Hill, is a direct heir of the expansive Hume, and appropriately there is a direct view between the two buildings. Stewart becomes in the next generation a great synthesiser of the Enlightenment endeavour to understand nature and human life as one comprehensive whole, applying his own special sensitivity to moral character and psychology.

Stewart's contribution to progressive thought is dealt with elsewhere in this volume, but he also draws attention to our ability to imagine that things may have been different from how they are now. He calls this 'conjectural history', and David Hume was one of its practitioners. Society in the past, they conjecture, was different from what we take for granted now. In fact, even today, different cultures may have very different values and ways of seeing. In Scotland itself, at that time, the Highland and Lowland worlds still seemed alien to each other. Perhaps in the future, things may be different from the past or present. This gift of imagining things other than as they appear is liberating and a force for change, which is how one could describe Hume's intellectual legacy.

Among Dugald Stewart's admiring students was the young Walter Scott. He went on to develop the historical novel for exactly this kind of imagining. Moreover he also combines a devotion to character and psychology with a shrewd sense of social or historical change. Through Stewart, Scott and many others of his generation imbibed both the histories and the philosophy of the Enlightenment, keeping the stream flowing through the nineteenth as well as the 18th century. It is worth also noting that Dugald Stewart was very supportive of Robert Burns, when the young Ayrshire poet faced the hard task of trying to break into Edinburgh's cultural scene.

Coming back to Hume himself, we remember that his happiest years were spent settled in Edinburgh, reading, writing and conversing with fellow authors and thinkers. When terminally ill, probably with cancer of the stomach, Hume claimed he was most contented and at peace with himself. In his last months, the philosopher penned a short autobiography that is as restrained and ordered as his memorial. It is also a classic of Scottish prose:

> It is difficult for a man to speak long of himself without Vanity: therefore I shall be short. It may be thought an instance of Vanity, that I pretend at all to write my Life: but this Narrative shall contain little more than the History of my Writings; as indeed almost all my Life has been spent in literary Pursuits and Occupations. The first success of most of my writings was not such as to be an Object of Vanity.

So, with wry self-deprecation, Hume recalls how his philosophic masterpiece 'A Treatise of Human Nature... fell dead-born from the press'. Not even the religious zealots cottoned on or made a murmur!

However, the amiable and resigned Hume was not to be left in peace since in 1776, even while he lay equably dying, and happily reading, the irremediable James Boswell came calling. Boswell, who has left us literally millions of words of diaries, journals and letter, was not a man 'who could speak short of himself', but in the process he has left an unparalleled record of his times.

Boswell describes Hume as 'just a-dying', reclining in his drawing room in St David's Street, in a scratch wig and 'lean, ghastly and quite of an earthy appearance'. It was Boswell's custom to doorstep celebrities in search of both personal kudos and copy. But this visit is not akin to his bearding of Rousseau or Voltaire in their dens. It is a Sunday morning and what is on Boswell's mind is religion. Throughout his journals, Boswell displays an almost morbid fixation with death and salvation, alongside a very unpresbyterian compunction to exhibit remorse, indulge in elaborate confessions and abase himself before the Almighty – until the next binge at least.

This particular Sunday he is too late for church and goes round to Hume instead. 'He seemed to be placid and even cheerful,' observes the puzzled diarist, who 'I know not how' contrives to get the conversation worked round to the subject of 'immortality'. Hume recounts his present lack of belief calmly, while acknowledging his religious upbringing and the role of religion in moderating the passions. He then goes on to criticise the morality of organised religion.

Boswell proceeds to defend religion light heartedly and to joke about meeting Hume in a future life. At the same time, he is shivering with delighted horror at such infidel levity – on the Sabbath, no less! In classic Boswell mode, the guest begins to internalise the scepticism of his host and to doubt his own state of faith. It is vintage Boswell but at the same time points up Hume's integrity of character and his courage in the face of death. As Boswell himself records, 'death for the time did not seem dismal'. Yet the diarist departed, disturbed in mind, and returned to this account several times adjusting and adding to it. In consequence we have this unusually intimate portrait of the last days of a great philosopher, who remains one of Edinburgh's presiding spirits.

Take a moment to stand at the gate of Hume's modest monument and reflect on his significance in a world where ill-tempered slanging matches and intolerant ideologies mar a period much in need of some rational self-questioning and enlightened dialogue. Can we hear a sigh or even a wry 'I told you so' in the quiet interior? Perhaps the Humean shade is comforted by the glorious view up to Calton Hill where the limpid beauty of Dugald Stewart's classical monument meets the eye, serenely connecting with its philosophical inspiration.

John Commonweal – Pillar of the Folk

James Boswell, the indefatigable diarist, also wrote about Calton Hill. But in his day, and Hume's, the hill and its immediate environs were not associated with philosophy but with the more volatile passions. Boswell himself, in his periodical outbursts of dissipation, sought out prostitutes on Calton Hill, and the nearness of the unlit Hill to the night time city has made it an attractive locale for sexual encounters through the centuries. By the middle of the last century, Calton Hill was particularly associated with gay liaisons.

Though Calton Hill is designated as a public park it is still a relatively unconfined space. In fact the boundaries were only defined by the construction of the flanking Georgian terraces. So again the openness, combined with its central location, makes the Hill an ideal place of assembly and protest. The Radical Tour in this volume outlines a Calton tradition which has now been partially displaced by the Holyrood Parliament as the desired destination for marches and protests.

Given this background of licence and protest, it is surely no accident that two prisons were built on the southern slope. The Calton Jail, which was designed by Archibald Elliot, replaced the overcrowded and squalid High Street Tolbooth in 1817. It incorporated an earlier Bridewell, or women's prison, which had been designed by Robert Adam. Lord Cockburn later criticised the whole idea of locating prisons on such a glorious landmark, but the authorities were determined to reclaim the Hill for the forces of order, and if necessary repression, at a time of political unrest.

In fact, Elliot's design tried to accommodate the picturesque with ramparts and castellated Gothic, from which the solitary Governor's Tower eccentrically survives, sometimes mistaken by disorientated tourists for the Castle. But viewed from the south Elliot's massive retaining wall, bastioned and bulwarked, undergirding the prisons, is prominently visible, though now propping up the government offices in St Andrews House. This southern rampart echoes the hubris with which Waterloo Bridge monumentally joins Calton Hill to the New Town streetscape. Nature was to be confined and conquered.

None of these architectural niceties could conceal the harshness of 19th century prison regimes, and the bare discomfort of these institutions. On a darker note the prisons continued another longstanding role of Calton Hill as a place of execution. Again Cockburn railed against the barbarity of public executions on Calton Hill. Here criminals, sorcerers and witches had been traditionally burnt for centuries, and after the erection of the new prison it was proposed that the jail would provide a very convenient viewing platform for spectators on the hill to witness hangings – which was at one time a popular Edinburgh pastime. Thankfully this barbaric spectacle was averted, but when public executions were finally abandoned later in the 19th century, Calton Jail became the place of judicial execution.

Fortunately other kinds of spectacle were traditionally on offer in Edinburgh and Calton Hill continued to be an ideal location. The ancient Fire Festival of Beltane has been revived as a dramatic masque in modern times, and torchlit processions to the Hill form part of the city's revived Hogmanay celebrations. The emphasis of these events is on popular participation rather than professional performance.

The same applies to the tournaments, archery contests and military exercises that were encouraged by the Stewart monarchs on the Greenside slope of Calton Hill to raise the general level of fitness and military preparedness of the citizenry in a country with no standing army. But it was as a play green that Greenside came into its own,

through the centuries when theatre was primarily an outdoor spectacle. It was here in 1554 that Scotland's great late medieval drama, *Ane Satyre of the Thrie Estaitis* was staged for the general public.

Had it not been for this remarkable event at Calton Hill – the play was also staged in Cupar – we would have known very little about early Scottish theatre. A few years later the Scottish Reformation put an end to drama as public entertainment, though unrecorded folk drama and school play readings continued. We are only now coming to terms with the full scope of Sir David Lindsay's masterpiece since it is a six-hour monumental marrying of different forms of theatre. The Edinburgh International Festival's 1948 revival, and most succeeding productions until the full re-enaction at Linlithgow in 2013, reduced the piece to a manageable morality play. But to imagine the full six-hour spectacle on Calton Hill is to bring many aspects of cultural life, and of this location, to vigorous life.

First, as a Scots speaking Fife laird, Lindsay was fully at home in the vernacular and bawdy comic tradition of folk theatre. At several points, such as the Interlude, Lindsay gives this style free rein with knockabout humour and sexual invective. These passages need to be seen and heard rather than read but it must have been decided that Edinburgh Festival audiences would expect something more refined from the City of Enlightenment. So, contrary voices such as this from the Pauper were excised:

> I will not give for all your play worth an sowis fart
> For there is richt little play at my hungrie heart.

Nonetheless, Lindsay's bawdy is interspersed within a Morality play format. The Virtues and Vices compete for influence on Rex Humanitas, the young king who is easily swayed in the wrong directions, particularly by Dame Sensualitie. This is the conventional medieval mainstream, but given added spice or bite, because everyone in the audience knew that Lindsay, formerly Lord Lyon Herald at the Scottish Court, had tutored the late King James v when he was young, and that the same monarch had been notorious for his free ranging sexual mores. The morality of court life under the current Queen Regent, James' widow Marie de Guise, was a hot issue as Protestant Reformers sought to undermine this determinedly Roman Catholic ruler. Lindsay's position in these arguments, and even James' intentions in allowing the first version of the play to be performed at Court more than a decade before, remain uncertain. The playwright was at the least sympathetic to the cause of reform, if not to the wholesale abandonment of traditional Catholicism.

These political and religious struggles provide the setting for yet another layer in the compendious multilayered drama. A Scots Parliament – the Thrie Estaitis – is summoned within the play to sort out the poor condition of the realm, but in a satiric masterstroke, the opening procession arrives 'gangin backwart'. This ushers in a detailed political debate with conservative and reforming forces battling it out over poverty, justice, church reform and good governance. A detailed list of measures is approved in a documentary style that anticipates modern political theatre by a few centuries. The idea of Calton Hill as a place of political assembly is also foreshadowed with this extraordinary, enacted parliament.

Within this section of the play, Lindsay plays another of his trump cards. John Commonweal arrives in rags to demand admittance to the parliament, even though he has no right to attend, as he belongs neither to the church hierarchy, the aristocracy or the burgh councils. In this scene the voice of democracy finds perhaps its earliest European expression, speaking directly to the monarch:

JOHN

Out of my gait! For God's sake let me gae!

Tell me, gude maister, again whit ye say.

DILIGENCE

I warn all that be wrongously offendit,

Come and complain and they sall be amendit...

What is they name, fellow? That wad I feil.

JOHN

Forsooth they call me John the Common-Weal.

Gude maister, I wad speir at you ane thing-

Where traist ye sall I find yon new-made King?

DILIGENCE

Come over and I will show thee to his grace.

JOHN

God's benison licht in that lucky face!

Stand by the gait; let see if I can loup.

I maun rin fast, in case I gat ane coup

(*Heir sall John loup the ditch, or fall in it*)

KING

Show me thy name, gude man, I thee command.

JOHN

Marry, John the Common-Weal of fair Scotland.

KING (*looking at John's rags*)

The Common-Weal has been amang his faes.

JOHN

Yea, sir. That gars the Common-Weal want claes!

KING

What is the cause the Common-Weal is cruikit?

JOHN

Because the Common-Weal has been overlukit.

KING

What gars thee look sae with ane dreary heart?

JOHN

Because the Thrie Estaitis gangs all backwart.

Having established his credentials, John Commonweal makes a prominent contribution to the debate, championing the cause of the 'Poor Man' against the privileged elites that constitute the Estates of Parliament.

The concept of 'commonweal' or 'commonwealth' was also prominent in the Scottish reformation of 1560, and has run through Scottish political and parliamentary debate since. A 'common weal' agenda for social and economic equality, developed by the Jimmy Reid Foundation, is influential in the current debate on Scottish independence. It is fair to say that the entrance of John Commonweal into the public debate on morality and government struck a chord in Scotland that resonates as strongly today as when first struck. Again, the public play green at Calton Hill seems the ideal location for this speech, given subsequent political events.

Finally, though, Sir David Lindsay, Lyon Herald, was a much travelled diplomat and an artist of European stature and sophistication. He chooses to finish his play with a farcical upending of all the serious characters and ideas entertained over the previous five and a half hours. This requires a virtuoso turn from a professional Fool, and one wonders if Lindsay had a particular performer in mind for this important part. Does his counterintuitive ending display a streak of worldly cynicism or just the instinct for a truly dramatic and exuberant finale? Or both?

Either way, at the close Lindsay takes the performance physically back to the audience, as if challenging us to learn something from his play or just to continue as before like a bunch of asses. Maybe our relieved enjoyment of the humorous finale is a touch uneasy!

It is a sad irony that when religious and social reform came in Scotland it led to the suppression of theatre, and a 400 year gap before *Ane Satyre of the Thrie Estaitis* would be performed again. Drama in general went underground and back into the folk tradition, while political theatre had to await its 20th century renaissance, with Theatre Workshop and 7:84 Theatre picking up where Lindsay left off. The only part of the original performance which was to continue without interruption was the public hanging of the Vices, which is portrayed with a characteristic Scots relish. But through all these refractions of theatre, Calton Hill continued to play a significant part in the urban and national drama.

Admiral Nelson – Pillar of Empire

The summit of Calton Hill is the ideal spot to view the engineering of Edinburgh. Formed from one volcanic landscape the city comprises a mix of hills, gullies and more gentle slopes. Essential to the development of a spacious New Town, north of the crowded Old Town ridge, are the North and South Bridges, spanning the ravines, and the artificial mound which created a descent from Old to New.

Subsequent to the Bridges, another link was proposed, spanning the gully between the New Town and Calton Hill. Begun in 1815, the same year that the foundation stone of Calton Jail was laid, the inevitably titled 'Waterloo Bridge' proved the most expensive of all Edinburgh's major engineering projects until the 21st century reinstatement of trams. The massive construction, which sliced through the Old Calton Burial Ground and completely overshadows the original route by Leith Street, was designed by Robert 'Lighthouse' Stevenson, grandfather of the famous Robert Louis.

This reshaped landscape has an avowedly imperial impact. A massive statue of the Duke of Wellington, victor of Waterloo, dominates the junction between North Bridge, Waterloo Place and Princes Street. The bridge conceals itself with two sets of triumphal arches commemorating Britain's victory over Napoleon and his French Empire. The intended effect is of a grand classical route leading towards Calton Hill. But to what end?

Rewind to an earlier and equally decisive victory over Napoleon, the sea Battle of Trafalgar on 21 October 1805. Within weeks of the famous victory, which was marred by Admiral Nelson's death, Edinburgh's great and good had convened to plan the first memorial in Great Britain to the fallen hero. This was an outpouring of imperial Britishness and a recognition of the importance of the Firth of Forth as a Royal Navy base.

A preliminary design by the artist Alexander Nasmyth was rejected, on grounds of cost, and supplanted with a design by Robert Burn. The resultant one hundred foot 'rustic' tower has been frequently lampooned because of its supposed resemblance to Nelson's upturned telescope. Whatever the design's inspiration, the usual funding problems plagued the venture, delaying work for eight years, and by the time the tower was completed in 1816, Robert Burn had died.

Notwithstanding these problems, the Nelson Monument is a salient reminder of Scotland's active involvement in the British Empire's first

global conflict. Though the Napoleonic wars were about hegemony in Europe, and a clash of political philosophies, they were a global struggle for territorial influence and trade. During key years of this extended conflict, Britain spent two thirds of its national income on the French wars, which were effectively the first world conflict.

In 1805 the final victory at Waterloo in 1815 was a long way off, and Napoleon threatened an invasion of Britain. Only the Royal Navy stood in the way of a French triumph. At 6.00am on 21 October, Nelson heard that the combined French and Spanish fleet of 33 warships under Admiral Villeneuve had left port at Cadiz. Though he had only 27 ships in his fleet, Nelson decided that this was the moment to strike and the British fleet set sail to join battle off Cape Trafalgar in southern Spain.

Normally sea battles were fought in this period by lining up the opposing fleets broadsides on so that maximum fire power could be brought to bear, only closing in after one or other ship was disabled. Instead Nelson adopted a radical tactic which had been devised by a Scottish Enlightenment intellectual, John Clerk of Eldin, in his 1782 'Essay on Naval Tactics'. This involved attacking the enemy line in columns with the aim of cutting through and rounding back, so disrupting the command signals and engaging from the vulnerable rear.

So, on the day, Nelson divided the British fleet into two columns – Weather and Lee – placing the fastest ships at the front, including his own flagship, *The Victory*. Though bold, this battle plan was also very dangerous for as the attacking ships approached the opposing line, and until they had broken through, they were exposed to the full force of hostile cannon fire at close range. Nelson, himself, was under no illusions about the risks, placing the flagships at the front to meet the greatest danger. After the first exchange of fire, he commanded closer engagement, directing *The Victory* herself into the centre of the French line where it fought three French ships at close quarters. Nelson remained on deck, refusing to take shelter.

Nelson's initiative and personal courage as commander won the day, but cost the Admiral his own life. Though the French line closed to support its embattled centre, the British fleet repulsed their counter-attack and most of the French and Spanish ships surrendered. Nelson had been carried below decks having been struck in the chest by a musket ball from the French flagship, *The Redoutable*, at 1.35pm, reportedly saying to the *The Victory's* Captain, 'They have done for me at last, Hardy'. At 4.15pm, Captain Hardy came below to confirm the battle had been won. An hour later Nelson was dead, having uttered the words, 'Now I am satisfied. Thank God I have done my duty'. This proved true not just for the day but for the overall war, since from that time the threat of a French invasion receded and British supremacy at sea was firmly established.

The Battle of Trafalgar is a milestone in war reportage as there are an exceptional number of eyewitness accounts from both sides, and the conflict was unexpected, dramatic, bloody, and long lasting in its consequences. However, within the top line story of the fight, there are many other narratives which link back to the Calton Hill Monument, some of which are recounted in the onsite exhibition.

One is the famous signal flown by Nelson from *The Victory* on the morning of the battle, and still flown from the Nelson Monument every Trafalgar Day. 'England expects every man will do his duty', a command echoed by Nelson's own last words – 'I have done my duty'. Of course a significant proportion of the sailors were Irish, Welsh and Scots, perhaps disproportionately so. There were over 60 Scots serving on *The Victory* itself while the overall fleet boasted five Scottish Captains and one

Rear-Admiral, William Carnegie, the Earl of Northesk. One of the two British commanders killed at Trafalgar, Captain Duff, was an Edinburgh man who lies buried at Nelson's feet in St Paul's Cathedral. So one story has a Scots wag responding to his fellow's complaint about the signal with, 'Aye, but he kens the Scots'll no let him doun onyroads'.

The Battle of Trafalgar was truly a Great British endeavour, harnessing all the material and human resources of the growing empire to defeat its global rival. Constructing, manning and supplying the Royal Navy was an industrial scale enterprise involving more than 500 ships, and up to 100,000 men. Fuelling the war effort drove technological and agricultural advances of necessity rather than choice. Much of the huge quantities of sail required were manufactured in Dundee, cannon balls came from the Bonawe Furnace in Argyll, while the devastatingly effective carronades, loaded with double shot and a crate of musket balls, were produced at the Carron Ironworks near Falkirk.

But if the material cost of the victory was enormous, the human cost was truly atrocious. Official records suggest that in this one day of conflict, nearly 5,000 died with a further 3,000 wounded. This is almost certainly an underestimate, since many of those subjected to medical treatment would have subsequently died. Taken below decks, the injured were dosed with alcohol and then musket balls and shrapnel were extracted or limbs amputated with knives and saws on bloodied tables. Those who survived the trauma and blood loss often succumbed to gangrene, while those who survived were horribly maimed for life. Nelson himself was treated below decks in the same conditions by an Irish-Scottish surgeon to whom he reputably said, 'My pain is so severe that I devoutly wish to be gone', which must have been a majority view.

Who were the dead and maimed? There were many volunteers but also press ganged conscripts. The war effort required quite literally human cannon fodder, and this was provided by 'the lower orders'. This overwhelming need for manpower also drove political repression since national security trumped democratic dissent through an extended period of war. Dissenters were easily painted as traitors when foreign invasion threatened.

'Manpower', however, is not the whole story. There were many children on board, especially the boys called 'powder monkeys' who ran from the stores to the guns with a continual supply of gun powder. John Doig from Leith, aged ten, was the youngest of them to serve at Trafalgar. Many ships also carried a quotient of officially five women, described, sometimes honorifically, as 'wives'. They also helped to service the guns and assisted the surgeons with the wounded. A Dundonian, Mary Buick, was responsible for embalming Admiral Nelson's body and preserving it in a cask of brandy to get it home for his state funeral. Laid out on a royal barge, Nelson's pickled remains were transported along the Thames to be solemnly interred at St Paul's Cathedral. Nelson's mistress, Emma Hamilton, insisted on exhibiting the fallen hero's bloodied uniform on the end of her bed, as she lay prostrate with grief receiving visitors.

The immediate aftermath, however, did not exhaust the human costs. Many were reduced to beggary by their injuries and eked out a miserable resistance as disabled people on the margins of a not very compassionate society. Dependents were also largely left to fend for themselves. In addition, many French sailors and marines who surrendered at Trafalgar were to spend long years as prisoners of war in Edinburgh Castle to where they could be conveniently delivered by sea through Leith.

Though the Nelson Monument was the first to be proposed in Britain, a typically Edinburgh wrangle about funding delayed its completion until 1816. Even then it took Robert Stevenson's professional intervention to convince the Town Council that the half-built tower was a danger to the public. The site was chosen because Calton Hill was already a naval mast and flag signalling station, and the proposed tower was always seen as having a dual function as both a memorial and a practical aid to navigation.

Before radar, ascertaining a ship's longitude was essential to navigation, but this depended on knowing the exact time, which was why ships carried quite sophisticated chronometers. The Calton Hill signals were needed to show ships in the Firth of Forth the time, and in 1818 Captain Robert Wauchope, a scion of the longstanding lairds of Niddrie, worked out that a visual time ball would be a better signal cue than a striking clock, since light travels faster than sound.

Charles Piazzi Smyth, Director of the City Observatory, had seen such a time ball in action in South Africa and in 1852 he followed through in Edinburgh, linking a time ball on top of the Nelson Monument to an electric clock in the Observatory. This was further improved in response to foggy conditions when a one o'clock gun, fired from the Castle, was instituted, originally linked to the Observatory clock by a 1.2 km long overhead wire. Minus the wire, this arrangement continues today with gun and time ball, though navigation has progressed in a different direction on the basis of James Clerk Maxwell's discovery that magnetic fields, sound waves and lights are a unified set of phenomena.

In this regard the Pillar of Empire sits on Calton Hill alongside the Pillar of Science. Nelson's Monument involves both, though within a decade of its completion plans were laid for an even more ambitious war memorial, which came to be called the Parthenon or, alternatively, 'Edinburgh's Disgrace'.

James Hutton to Clerk Maxwell – Pillar of Science

'Modern Athens Displayed', which is a prospectus for Edinburgh as the 'Athens of the North' published in 1829, describes the view from Calton Hill as follows:

> From the east end of Waterloo Place a flight of broad steps leads to the foot-path which winds round the Calton Hill. In traversing this, the spectator views in succession, the endless range of streets which compose the New Town, bounded by the Corstorphine Hills; the Firth of Forth, with the distant mountains; the Town and Harbour of Leith; Musselburgh Bay terminated by North Berwick Law; Arthur's Seat, and Salisbury Crags, with Holyrood House in the plain beneath; and lastly the darkened masses of the Old Town, skirted and guarded on one side by the ancient Citadel.

This view is an exercise in the picturesque but also the geological prospectus of a landscape much less built up than the one we see today, though the key landmarks remain before our eyes, substantially unchanged.

What we survey from Calton Hill is one mighty post-volcanic landscape ground down by ice and sea over millions of years. Arthur's Seat is a double vent. The Castle Rock and Calton Hill are both 'crag and tail' features caused by ice moving from the west, meeting the resistance of the crag which then catches a tail of debris, forming the gentler eastern slopes. Salisbury Crags is an extended volcanic sill, Princes Street Gardens a channel gouged out by the ice, the Pentlands an immense lava flow and so on. Climbing the steps from Waterloo Place you can see the holes through which the gases and vapours escaped from the cooling lava, filled as the liquids solidified.

This is now an accepted geological story but it was James Hutton, an 18th century Scottish Enlightenment thinker, who crafted this narrative by establishing the immense age of the earth, allowing for aeons of geological time before humanity peopled the globe. Hutton was a gentleman farmer, who came to live on St John's Hill in Edinburgh, in full view of Calton Hill and Arthur's Seat, in order to devote his life to establishing his theory of the earth. This landscape and its unusual features were key to Hutton's thinking, and although it was only in later life, when he was already failing, that Hutton finally put pen to paper on the overall theory, his outline of events has never been seriously challenged since. The modest 'amateur' had claimed a place amongst the giants of scientific achievement including Scottish contemporaries such as Joseph Black the chemist and James Gregory the physician.

So, on Calton Hill we are viewing a scientific landscape, in two senses. Firstly, what we see is the outcome of a long natural evolution, but the Hill also celebrates many of those who have investigated and explained the evolution of life as well as the physical sciences. It is in itself a monument to scientific achievement in one of its most fruitful and revolutionary periods. However, as Hume would remind us, the course of science is governed by human nature and is unlikely to be a smooth or uninterrupted ascent. And so it is with Calton Hill, as David Gavine of 'Scotland's Cultural Heritage Unit' discovered on researching the City Observatories.

The struggle commenced with the brilliant young mathematician, Colin Maclaurin, who petitioned the Town Council, as patrons of the University, to provide an observatory, arguing that the use of small telescopes was inadequate to the burgeoning experimental exploration of the night skies, and that the observations garnered would aid both navigation and trade. The latter was a shrewd pitch at the mercantile elite which ran Edinburgh. Unfortunately, the Porteous Riots of 1736 and the Jacobite Risng of 1745, when Maclaurin broke his health trying fruitlessly to devise defences against Bonnie Prince Charlie, thwarted the professor's best efforts.

It was not until 1776 that the arrival of the optician Thomas Short with a 12 foot reflecting telescope that interest was reignited. On the University's initiative, Short was granted a 99-year lease of half an acre near the summit of Calton Hill and a foundation stone was laid with due civic and academic ceremony.

At this juncture, Edinburgh's near fatal predilection for architectural dispute came into play. This was after all the first permanent building to be erected on the Hill. James Craig, who produced the master ground plan for the New Town, designed a 48-foot high octagonal tower for the telescope, with adjacent pavilions for the secondary instruments. As Craig's design took physical shape, Robert Adam intervened to suggest that a more gothic treatment would be better in this location with fortress style embrasures and buttresses echoing the castle. The builders changed direction, but by the time they had added the buttresses and embrasures to Craig's Tower, the bequest that poor Maclaurin had left in his will for an Observatory ran out, and the Town Council lost interest.

Things now descended into farce as Short occupied the building as a domestic house, constructing a temporary telescope shelter nearby. When he died in 1788 the lease passed to his grandson, a sailor called Douglas who petitioned the Council for funds. But Short's widow disputed the inheritance, removed parts of the telescope and then, infuriated by the eviction of her children by Douglas, mounted an armed assault, which left both the warring factions in jail. Douglas eventually returned to sea, perhaps as a teacher of navigation, and the 'Observatory' further declined ending up by 1807 as a gunpowder store.

In 1811, the newly formed Astronomical Institute of Edinburgh was established by a group of Edinburgh gentlemen, and adopted the aim of founding an observatory. The main purpose was to gather observations for navigation and to provide a time service for the Port of Leith which would enable ship's captains to set their chronometers. The mathematician and physicist, Professor John Playfair, headed the project which included many luminaries including Robert Stevenson the engineer and David Brewster, the prominent scientist and inventor. The Prince Regent graciously agreed to be patron, showing that this was truly an imperial as well as a learned venture. The Town Council, University, Trinity House, Royal Society and the Faculty of Advocates were all on board as trustees in a unified effort by Edinburgh's elites. To crown all in 1822, on his state visit to Edinburgh, the Prince Regent, now George IV, christened the venture 'the Royal Observatory'.

All this pomp and circumstance, however, did not wholly deliver the goods. The site was purchased and the new – now City – Observatory was built to a fine classical design by William Playfair. He incorporated a memorial to his mathematical Uncle John. But funds to provide the necessary equipment were lacking. Things dragged on until a Treasury grant was secured and finally in 1833 Thomas Henderson, an extremely competent practical astronomer was appointed, and began the work of amassing a bank of useful observations.

Meantime, however, Thomas Short's daughter Maria arrived to lay claim to her father's instruments, which were held by the Town Council. Such was the legal tangle still surrounding the original Observatory that the Council allowed her to set up a wooden 'popular observatory' nearby behind the uncompleted National Monument, where she charged admission in conjunction with a display of 'national hero' statues and associated sideshows. Later Maria transferred her operation

to Castle Hill, establishing what later became the Outlook Tower and is now Camera Obscura.

In 1844, Thomas Henderson died to be replaced as Royal Astronomer by Charles Piazzi Smyth, and in 1847 the Astronomical Institution was wound up and the Observatory taken under direct control of the Treasury in London. James Craig's 'Gothic Tower' became an assistant astronomer's house. Smyth, however, was still also Professor of Astronomy at Edinburgh University. In effect neither organisation took much interest in his work, leaving him perpetually complaining about a lack of time to both teach and observe, while the poor state of the instruments constantly hampered progress.

Nonetheless Piazzi Smyth was a brilliant astronomer and an individualist who made his mark in a variety of directions, not always grounded in his immediate practical duties. From his official residence in Royal Terrace, Smyth made a series of pioneering studies of the Aurora Borealis and luminous night clouds. His interest in atmospheric conditions led Smyth to experiment with observations from higher altitudes, above cloud level and free from the smokes of Auld Reikie. He famously spent his honeymoon with his Edinburgh-born wife Jessie Duncan in 1856 on a mountain top in Tenerife, and can fairly be called the father of mountain observatories. Navigation was not neglected and the time ball was installed on the Nelson Monument so that mariners could set their chronometers in the Firth of Forth rather than bringing them up to the Observatory.

Piazzi Smyth was interested in all the effects of light, and an expert photographer. Through his measurement of heat from the moon he became a pioneer in the field of infra-red astronomy. He had an obsession with the Egyptian Pyramids and believed that they were designed according to a system of as yet unrealised mathematical harmonies that lay behind the physical laws of the universe. In pursuit of this system he surveyed the Great Pyramid at Giza using an ingenious system of trolleys and cameras. When the Royal Society of Edinburgh refused to publish the results of his researches he resigned as a Fellow.

The troubles with government funding however rumbled on, despite a Royal Commission in 1876 recommending new investment. Finally a larger telescope was installed under a second iron dome but Piazzi Smyth's insistence that this needed to be located on a mountain top was ignored. He retired to the Lake District to study clouds. Except perhaps on the pyramids, Piazzi Smyth's intuitions and investigations were to prove fruitful on nearly every count and he deserves an honoured place in Edinburgh's scientific story.

The future of the City Observatory was more mixed. On the initiative of the Earl of Crawford, a new Royal Observatory was opened on Blackford Hill in 1896 and astronomy was properly established as a University course. That institution still flourishes though fed by observations from radio telescopes on a Hawaii mountain top. The Calton Hill Observatory continued under the auspices of the City Council, and flourished for a while on the strength of its 22 inch reflecting telescope, before once more subsiding into neglect and finally disuse. Current plans will see the buildings restored as an art gallery.

The scientific achievements, however, went on. James Clerk Maxwell, who went to school in Edinburgh, took up spectroscopy, the investigation of light, and then electro-magnetism, finally connecting these phenomena in a brilliant set of mathematical equations. In moving beyond the mechanistic world of Newtonian physics into field theories, Maxwell paved the way for 20th century technologies and Einstein's theory of relativity. Alexander Stoddart's superb statue of James Clerk Maxwell is sited at the east end of George Street – the sitting figure looks towards Calton Hill where the ground breaking scientific genius played as a boy.

Innovation and scientific discovery continue in Edinburgh with its most recent accolades accorded to Peter Higgs after whom the indescribably small sub-atomic particle, the Higgs Boson, is named. We can still look out from Calton Hill on a city of science, and remember some of the pioneers, whose eccentricities add rather than detract from their appeal. Scientists too are human, and their discoveries form part of humanity's struggle to understand both ourselves and our place in the universe. Enlightenment is ongoing.

Robert Burns – Pillar of Democracy

The Martyr's Monument in the Old Calton Burial Ground is the most prominent pillar to radical political thought and action on the Hill. It represents both the struggle for 'representation of the people' through the years of conflict after the French Revolution but also the subsequent reform movements that gradually extended the franchise. In 1832, before the first Reform Act, an electorate of 30 people appointed Edinburgh's MPs. But the Monument does not exhaust the story of democratic values. This requires a walk to the Burns Monument on Regent Road, and some sightseeing in between.

St Andrews House was erected as a government office on the foundations of the Calton Jail. It was closed in the 1920s when Saughton Prison was built on the western edge of the city. A department of the Westminster Government devoted to Scotland had been established by Prime Minister Gladstone in 1885, with a Scottish

Secretary in the Cabinet. This was intended to enable Scotland a parallel measure of Devolution as Home Rule for Ireland looked a likely development. However, the administration of the Scottish ministry remained in Whitehall, and Irish Home Rule stalled. By the 1920s, Ireland (minus the partitioned north) had been, in the parlance of the time, 'lost to the Empire'. Government functions were divided across London and Edinburgh, so it was decided to move the Scottish Office to Edinburgh and counter the growth of a modern nationalist movement with a substantial edifice on Calton Hill.

This diplomatic measure of administrative Devolution ran into immediate trouble, since the Ministry of Works in London proceeded to commission an office building in the normal Whitehall manner and style. A very Edinburgh rumpus ensued demanding a Scottish architect for this prominent site and iconic building. Soon everyone from the Moderator of the Church of Scotland to Queen Mary was involved, and a Scottish Committee had to be established to select an architect and the design.

The resultant edifice, designed by Thomas Tait, is an ingenious mix of classicism and art deco. On the south side it makes a brilliant use of the Calton Jail's massive retaining walls, allowing the building to climb the rock face in a series of levels. But despite some softening touches of detail and decoration, the principle façade seems clinical and detached. Something of the jail lingered. There is even in retrospect a slightly chilling resemblance to the 1930s architecture of fascism, and indeed the offices were formally opened within hours of the start of World War II.

Unfortunately, as the 20th century progressed, and the political choices of the Scottish and English electorates diverged, it was the undemocratic or closed face of government that came to prominence. That was why in 1992 the Democracy Vigil set up camp immediately opposite St Andrews House, challenging the legitimacy of the Scottish administration, and remained there until Scotland secured its own parliament in the 1997 Devolution vote.

But St Andrews House is not the principal building on Calton Hill or even on Regent Road. That accolade has to go to the Old Royal High School which looks squarely and magnificently from the Hill over to Arthur's Seat. It is the work of the architect Thomas Hamilton, who also designed the Burns Monument, and who is appropriately interred in the Old Calton Burial Ground. The school was completed in 1829, and was generously funded by the Council to be – and seen to be – Edinburgh's premier academy. Later, after the school was moved to Barnton, the building was prepared as the home for the not-to-be Scottish Assembly of 1979, and again in 1999, the Old Royal High School was touted as a home for the new Scottish Parliament, which went instead to Holyrood. Technically still called New Parliament House, Hamilton's masterwork is one of Edinburgh's finest buildings still in search of a worthy use.

But there is more to the Old Royal High School than its original function. This is the defining Scottish Greek Revival monument, underpinning Calton Hill's 'Acropolis' claim, and embodying Edinburgh as 'the Athens of the North'. Thomas Hamilton's design is inspired by Temple of Hephaestus which is close to the Agora or marketplace in Athens. This building is still popularly called the Theseion, due to an earlier mistaken belief that it was a shrine for the bones of Athens' hero King Theseus. But any talk of 'imitation' here seriously undervalues Hamilton's genius in matching prime features of the Athenian 'Theseion' to this dramatically different Edinburgh location. This building becomes a Scottish Temple to learning and democracy, sited commandingly in our distinctive landscape.

Hamilton was also influenced by the Athenian Acropolis and by its gateway temple. The Old Royal High School offers its own ceremonial gateway to Calton Hill as a whole. Not only does the facade rise in ascending levels, but the massive pedimented gateways on either side command a reverent entrance and ascent up the symmetrical stairs. The building not only works in its own right, but is also a unifying feature for the whole hilltop assembly of monuments.

Behind this lies a cluster of ideas linking the northern light and rigour of Scotland with the plainest style of Greek classical architecture, the Doric. The subtext is that in terms of philosophy, religion and politics Scotland emulates classical cultural achievements through its continuing Enlightenment. Even the tensions between Enlightenment and war, democracy and empire, that characterise Calton Hill harks back to the history of Athenian democracy and the imperial power accumulated by this greatest of the Greek city states.

Unfortunately, Calton Hill as a whole has not yet caught up with Thomas Hamilton's vision. The main access road up the hill awkwardly cuts the rear of the Old High School off from its setting. There is no direct relationship between the fine façade of the school or its magnificent internal features such as the central Debating Chamber, and the rest of Edinburgh's sacred mount. The problem is both visual and physical. To continue our democracy walk up the Hill you would have to backtrack and follow the access road, with its severely restricted views, up to the Vigil Cairn and finally the Parthenon. After the promise of the Doric Temple it is a real let down, only redeemed when you reach the actual summit with its superb panoramas.

So, instead, we will continue this walk along Regent Road towards the Burns Monument. The views from here across to Arthur's Seat and the Old Town are among the best in the city. Moreover, this is an excellent vantage point from which to see the relationship between the natural landscape, the Palace of Holyroodhouse and the new Scottish Parliament. The decision to build the parliament at the ancient seat of Scottish nationhood and royal power seems on reflection a strange one for the then Labour-Liberal Democrat Coalition intent on Devolution rather than independence. It may be that the undoubted artistic tastes of the first First Minister, Donald Dewar, swayed his political and financial caution. The end result, designed by the Spanish architect Enric Miralles, is a major historical statement with national and international resonances which are still being sounded.

The Burns Monument occupies its own knoll on the shoulder of Calton Hill, near the end of Regent Road. At first sight it seems a standard establishment monument, erected in a capital city which accorded Robert Burns himself a notoriously ambiguous reception. One need only look downwards from here to the Canongate Kirkyard to read the complexities. There, Burns' poetic hero Robert Fergusson was given a pauper's burial, till the Bard of Caledonia provided a headstone. There too, Agnes McLehose, the poet's middle class and therefore unattainable Clarinda is interred. But once again, Thomas Hamilton has not failed us in either vision or execution.

The interior of the Burns Monument is a pure cylindrical temple, with a perfectly proportioned colonnade. The roof seems to rest above with little visible support and the acoustic is outstandingly clean. This is a radical design and tribute from one great artist to another, and I for one am rather grateful that the Flaxman statue of Burns as 'the ploughman poet' which was commissioned for the Monument was moved to the Scottish National Portrait Gallery. Burns is a poet of the Enlightenment as well as of Romantic sensibility and the interior of Hamilton's design leaves space for all these aspects of Burns, the national and international artist, to resound and revolve in our minds.

The Burns Monument is inspired by the Choragic Monument of Lysicrates in Athens, as is the Dugald Stewart Monument which William Playfair later designed. But in Burns' case there is a special appropriateness in the link. Choragic monuments were raised in honour of those who funded the dramatic contests which were a prominent feature of Athenian festivals. The centerpiece of these Greek dramas, comedies and tragedies, was the chorus which required musical, movement and dramatic talent of a high order. Those winning the contests were awarded a sacred tripod, which features on the top of this Monument with supporting griffons.

There is a special irony and appropriateness in this tribute to Scotland's national poet. Robert Burns would have dearly liked to write for the Edinburgh Playhouse, and he was very friendly with the company there, especially the leading actor William Woods, who is also buried in the Old Calton graveyard. But the theatre conditions of the day precluded a peasant farmer writing on Scottish themes from being performed. The lairds and lawyers of Edinburgh would have greeted such a development with outraged horror. Later, in Dumfries, Burns did become involved with the new Theatre Royal and wrote some prologues for the stage, but he never fulfilled his undoubted dramatic ambitions and capabilities. His one surviving dramatic work, *Love and Liberty* or *The Jolly Beggars*, is an anarchic folk cantata which could not be published, far less performed, during the poet's lifetime. That masterpiece, along with the superbly dramatic 'Tam O' Shanter' show what might have been achieved.

So, by awarding Burns the tripod, Hamilton is making his own potentially subversive statement. It is also in the long run a true statement, since the poetry and songs of Robert Burns created a whole new platform for Scottish culture, national and international, which has outlasted all the theatres and stage plays of his time. The accolade is surely deserved.

However, given what we have learned about Thomas Hamilton's Calton Hill buildings, this Monument clearly has political and philosophical, as well as an artistic meaning. Just as the Greek dramatists underpinned and expressed the core values of Greek society, so Burns summed up in his art Scottish aspirations and values. Hamilton embodies these in the Monument, and by doing so comments on the whole ethos and purpose of the Hill and its various memorials. The architect's radical space is asking to be filled with the poet's radical words:

Is there, for honest poverty
That hangs his head, and aw that:
The coward slave, we pass him by,
We dare be poor for aw that!
For aw that, and aw that,
Our toils obscure, and aw that,
The rank is but the guinea's stamp,
The man's the gowd for aw that.

Yet these political and moral ideas are rooted in a fellowship of heart and head that, in Burns' view, unites humanity beyond any distinctions of class, wealth, race or creed. And that is why his international anthem of fellow feeling that still resounds globally:

Should auld acquaintance be forgot
And never brought tae mind,
Should auld acquaintance be forgot
And auld lang syne.

For auld lang syne, my jo,
For auld lang syne,
We'll tak a cup o' kindness yet
For auld lang syne.

David Octavius Hill – Pillar of Art

The 19th century Scottish artist, David Octavius Hill, was quite literally a pillar of the arts. Born in Perth, Hill was a landscape artist who responded visually to the poetry of Burns and the novels of Walter Scott with oil paintings and prints. But he was also a natural organiser and collaborator, becoming Secretary of the Royal Scottish Academy, and later the driving force behind the construction of the National Gallery of Scotland. Both of these classical galleries on the Mound, with their porticos and multiple pillars, owe a debt to Hill.

David Octavius Hill, like Robert Burns, was a consciously national artist, and in 1843 he was caught up in the drama of the Disruption of the Church of Scotland. Hill, like many of his Scottish contemporaries, saw the now largely forgotten exodus of ministers and congregations from the Presbyterian establishment as a movement for religious, political and cultural liberty. He conceived the idea of a dramatic canvas that would capture this moment of history, as Sir George Harvey had captured in a similarly epic canvas the passing at Westminster of the 1832 Reform Act, or Sir David Wilkie had sought to recreate the conflict of the 16th century reformation.

It was this ambition, combined with tragic personal events, which brought David Octavius Hill to Calton Hill. In 1841, Hill's wife Ann MacDonald died shortly after the birth, and early death, of their second child. Hill was left to bring up his surviving daughter, Charlotte. Soon afterwards, as Hill began to grapple with his Disruption painting, his friend David Brewster suggested using the new technique of photography in order to record the people who had participated in the Disruption drama. On Brewster's influential recommendation, a young photographer from St Andrews, Robert Adamson, set up a studio in Rock House on the south western side of Calton Hill, where the exposed light was ideal for the new technique. Though now a private house, Rock House is still clearly visible, with a later studio occupying the sheltered garden where many of the 'calotypes' were exposed. It is best seen from the front door of the Parliament Hotel on the street called Calton Hill, which links Leith Street and Waterloo Place by way of a steep climb.

Hill enthusiastically endorsed the calotype portraits, and as the labour of photographing all the Ministers got underway, the artist and his surviving daughter ended up moving into Rock House with Adamson. There the sunny sheltered garden, not to mention the wider spaces of Calton Hill, provided an ideal playground while Adamson and his assistant Miss Mann provided a surrogate family.

Quickly, Hill realised that the calotype process had artistic potential far beyond recording the Disruption clergy. He and Adamson began to photograph on location and to create costumed compositions in historic settings. From Calton Hill the social story of Scotland could be viewed at a glance. To the south, the slums of Edinburgh's Old Town showed the decay of the older communal society, and the huge pressures created by rapid urbanisation. Northwards the New Town exhibited a more divided and stratified society with the segregation of rich and poor. Yet on the Forth shore, the Free Fishers of Newhaven continued a co-operative communal lifestyle, still connected with the natural world. It was in response to these challenges that Thomas Chalmers, leader of the Disruption, had sought to restore traditional parish communities, even in the cities, first from within the Church of Scotland, and when that was thwarted by the House of Lords, through a new 'Free' Church.

While Adamson was technically accomplished, it was Hill who saw the potential of the new medium to portray a wider social and historical drama. With reborn enthusiasm, Hill's creative energy fuelled an outburst of work, directed from Rock House, that was to become a permanent benchmark not only for Scottish culture but for the art of photography. Tragically this intense period ended after only a few short years with the decline of Robert Adamson's health and his early death in 1848.

David Octavius Hill stayed on at Rock House but the creative impetus had gone, and he was left with a 20 year struggle to complete the monumental Disruption painting, which can still be viewed in the head office of the continuing Free Church of Scotland on the Mound. Unfortunately the finished product lacks the immediacy of the calotypes, or the fluid energy of Hill's drawings and paintings. That spontaneous moment in time had passed.

Sadly, Hill's beloved daughter Charlotte died like her mother Ann, after childbirth, in 1862. These heart rending events are the moving inspiration of David Octavius Hill's finest work *In Memoriam: Calton Hill* which was painted in 1862. The viewpoint is above Rock House looking down onto the Calton Jail and the receding urban landscape. On the left is a camera on its tripod and on the right an easel, commemorating the two arts of memory that Hill had practiced. But in the centre of the composition is the Old Calton Burial Ground, with the scattered tombs surrounding David Hume's and the Martyrs' Monuments. First Ann, then Adamson, and finally Charlotte and her baby.

Fortunately, 1862 was also the year in which Hill met and married the artist Amelia Paton. So commenced another creative partnership in Rock House on Calton Hill. Amelia actively encouraged completion of the Disruption epic (it was a very large canvas in a modest house!) and supported a new wave of her husband's work, while also practicing her own skills as a sculptor with his strong encouragement. So Rock House once again witnessed happiness and creative fulfillment, in a very

Edinburgh union, until ill-health forced retirement on Hill and a move to the more secluded Newington Lodge on the south side.

Together, David and Amelia tell us a great deal about the influence of the arts in 19th century Scotland, and their connection with society as a whole. The Calton Hill location points up a continuing Scottish Enlightenment with its dynamic linkage between science, arts and humane politics, and a religious spirit free of sectarian and ideological exclusions.

Memory Hill, a play produced for David Octavius Hill's bicentenary in 2002, imagines an elderly Hill meeting James Clerk Maxwell by chance walking on Calton Hill. They discuss Maxwell's ideas about colour photography but also the limitations of science, and art, in imitating the subtleties of nature. 'However far we move,' says Maxwell, 'Nature is always beyond us. It recedes and expands as we advance'. The living demonstration of this is around them on the Hill with its ever changing qualities of light.

'Everyone', suggests Maxwell, 'must build a bridge between what we know, and what we are in ourselves'. This paves the way for a quote from Clerk Maxwell's true life statement of the reverence, and the receptive imagination, which is the ground of fruitful innovation in all aspects of human knowledge and endeavour:

> I have always felt that what is done by 'myself' is done by something greater than myself, in me – something that eludes age and time.

With this sentiment, Hill the artist is in wholehearted accord, as were so many of those commemorated on Edinburgh's 'Memory Hill'.

Parthenon Pillars: An Epilogue

Something of the elusive quality evoked by David Octavius Hill and James Clerk Maxwell broods over the central monument on Calton Hill, the unfinished Parthenon. The project was originally conceived as a war memorial that would top both Waterloo Bridge and the Nelson Monument in honouring Scots who had died in the titanic global struggle with Napoleon. At first this was thought of as a church – perhaps similar in ethos to the National War Memorial built in Edinburgh Castle after World War I. But then Edinburgh's cultural ambitions came into play.

A committee of the Scottish great and good was formed around the idea of building a 'Parthenon' to crown Edinburgh's Acropolis Hill. Through this classical inspiration the pillars of war and empire could also be seen as a philosophical and scientific statement. The Committee's prospectus even claimed that their new Monument would endure when the Athenian Parthenon would have crumbled, which proved a rather fatal boast.

This style of thinking was advanced by the appointment of William Playfair as the architect. Playfair's roll of classical buildings in Edinburgh already included Old College, as conceived by Robert Adam, the Royal Scottish Academy, and the City Observatory on Calton Hill. Later he was to add the National Gallery of Scotland to his laurels. If pillars were needed, and on a grand scale, then Playfair was your man.

Edinburgh's Parthenon is indeed designed on a grand scale yet its massive monumentality is balanced by the simplicity and purity of its classical form. Unfortunately, it was also massively expensive, with up to 70 horses required to drag the huge sculpted blocks of Craigleith stone up to the site. Money ran out, and work ground to a halt. But perhaps there was more to it than these practical issues. The titanic struggle was over, the heat had gone out of the moment and something of the Promethean spirit, so evident on the Hill, had slowed or calmed. If the Parthenon had been completed, would its scale have been too dominant, too massive for Calton Hill and Edinburgh?

Of course the urge to complete the National Monument in some form continued. In 1832, a more populist approach arrived in the form of a Lanarkshire stonemason, Robert Forrest, who created a suite of 30 statues of 'national heroes' which were exhibited in a pavilion behind the one completed face of Playfair's classical temple. Forrest's five ton statues remained there till 1876 when they were dispersed after his death. During part of this period, Maria Short added her 'popular observatory', and Camera Obscura to the mix, cashing in on Calton Hill's popularity with locals and sightseers alike, as well as the growing Victorian entertainments industry.

Other proposals were advanced including converting the Monument into a National Gallery, running a funicular railway up to it, and so forth. The unfinished fragment was labelled 'Edinburgh's Disgrace' and there was a long running, albeit generalised, campaign to complete the work. In 1844 the popular stained glass artist and poet, James Ballantine, published an 'Address to Edinburgh' in his widely circulated *Gaberlunzie's Wallet*. The rousing climax of his exhortation is as follows:

> Awake my country, why delay?
> Ye slumber in the blaze of day,
> All shameless in your shame;
> To let this noble fragment stand
> A wreck, unfinish'd, and a brand
> Upon the Scottish name;

While strangers as they pass it by
Thus sneeringly deride –
'There stands old Scotland's Poverty,
And poor old Scotland's Pride.
Come start, men, show heart, men,
Be souls and sinew strain'd,
Till ample this temple,
Shall tell the conquest gain'd

Come forth with throbbing breasts and hearts,
Come forth like men and play your parts,
Come forth in patriot bands;
Let Highland heart and Lowland breast
Swell proudly as the mountain crest
On which this temple stands;
Resume your noble work of love,
Stint not your country's fame,
Until her glory gleams above
In characters of flame;
Then flourishing and nourishing
Art, science, love and peace,
Our north home shall forth come,
And rival ancient Greece!

In the 20th century, the campaign for a Scottish Parliament revived the idea of the Hill as a place of political Assembly, and the link was made between the Old Royal High School and the Parthenon. The contemporary Edinburgh architect Malcolm Fraser argued strongly for the Calton Hill buildings, including St Andrews House, as the best home for the restored Parliament. He envisaged the outline of the

Parthenon being completed, with an array of slender flags and flagpoles, contributed from schools across Scotland and blowing in the wind like Himalayan prayer flags. This also picks up on the Vigil Cairn with its stones from across Scotland and George Wylie's contemporary Stones of Scotland circle on Regent Road. It is certainly true that the political traditions of Calton Hill deserve recognition and celebration in some further public artwork.

However, some architectural writers, including A.J. Youngson, have argued that the Monument is in fact finished. Its incompleteness is more rewarding, and attractive than a perfect replica of the Athenian Parthenon could ever be. This appeals partly to the sense of a 'classical ruin', but not wholly, since Playfair's work does not look in any way ruined. The stronger effect is of a 'work in progress' that we are invited to imagine completing.

And in the end that is the most satisfying coping stone our Calton Hill of Monuments could have. It is a work unfinished that we are invited to complete, visually or in some kind of dramatic performance with the Monument as its backdrop. In the same way Scotland and its Enlightenment are ongoing, unfinished 'works in progress'. Playfair himself came to see his unfinished design as a thing of beauty and in proportion.

On Robert Burns Day 2000, the Royal Lyceum Youth Theatre performed a high energy dance routine on Edinburgh's day in the Millennium Dome. Called 'Light Assembly – On Calton Hill', it was accompanied by dramatic projected images of our city, and these words by the present writer:

> *Fire on the mountain, light on the hill*
> *Gainst castle rock the clouds are breaking*
> *North winds blow freedom from the sea.*

Panorama from the hill of old and new, firth and sky
Down dark closes, up terraced streets, fisherman and city slicker
Workers, lawyers, beggars, actors all in painter's eye
White wash of sun, a camera shutters close to see the light.

chorus

Stippled cityscape of stone, towers and steeples
Concepts in time, ideas of being, human liberty, equality
For aw that brought crashing down the pillars of destruction
Till monuments of war give way to parliaments of peace.

chorus

Mind goes deeper faster than a spinning axis
Gravity of planets gyre electric energy
Shake the kaleidoscope into its firework-coloured theatre
Light shifts across the universe now wave now particle in flight.

chorus

It all works together if we only can connect
Earth's story fired in fossil layers, the living cell
The helix gene that codes disease and healing power
This city's spirit and the body of its folk.

Fire on the mountain, light on the hill
Gainst castle rock the clouds are breaking
North winds blow freedom from the sea.

The Vigil

Heroes unsung
is a story aft tellt
mang vauntin
o conquest an triumph,
the advantage taen
bi the shair an the slick
wha hae nae room fur doubt
as if
aw tha wis needit
wis the firm hand
an a clear coorse;
the Vigil tellt itherwise
the scramblin
fur a steady thocht
in iver mair unchartit watters,
the need tae haud thegither
whan awthin
cried fur fracture
that
taught us deeper nor wards
for there
amang the fears an tears
an aw the complications
oor tribe cuid muster,
whit ran amang us
an rose abune us
the smoke o ae fire
stoked
wi the hairtsair certainty
that we

wid hae oor say
the wey we wantit
tae say it,
whiles.

A little magic and mystery

Although Calton Hill is rich in tradition regarding science, philosophy and history, the role of the hill has also long included an element of magic and mystery. It was one of the sites in the city associated with the great seasonal rituals of the past – a role which resonates today in the revived Beltane festival. However, unlike Arthur's Seat, there are not many extant stories of Calton Hill regarding the supernatural. There is, however, one particular tale that has echoes of some of the older beliefs concerning Arthur's Seat and other significant hills in Scotland and beyond. This story was originally reported in Richard Bovet's *Pandæmonium, or the Devil's Cloister Opened*, published in 1683. Bovet stressed how well-known and trustworthy Burton is; that he was a recognised figure in commercial circles in London, and that there was no need for Bovet to justify Burton's integrity. He then tells us that he is unsure of whether the Fairy Boy was recounting what was essentially a dream experience of some kind, or not, but then goes on to say that it was strange that the boy had run away considering he was given the temptation of wine and money to keep him there, noting that money and wine were a powerful temptation to lads of his age.

Back in the 1540s, an English sea-captain called Burton had brought his ship into Leith. This was a regular occurrence and he had had developed several friendships with local merchants in both Leith and Edinburgh, whom he would meet up with to socialise. One particular autumn evening, in a friend's house on the High Street over a few glasses of wine, Burton heard about a strange young orphan lad, no older than eleven, living on the streets of the city, who was called the Fairy Boy, and was said to have the gift of the 'second sight', being able to foretell the future. Burton had long been fascinated by the supernatural and arranged to have the lad brought round to the same house the following evening. He and his friends gathered again and the boy was brought in to meet them. Burton began to ply the lad with 'astrological' questions and soon realised that, though young, the fellow was both intelligent and informed. As the questions continued, the lad began to drum his fingers rhythmically on the table they were sitting at. Burton asked him if he could play the drum. The lad laughed and said, 'Och, aye, I can drum as well as any man in Scotland, for every Thursday night I beat all points to a great crowd of people that meet under yonder hill.' At this, he pointed out of the window at Calton Hill.

He went on to tell Burton that he would go into the hill through a great pair of gates which were invisible to normal people and that in a great hall under the hill, there would be all sorts of music and feasting. 'Sometimes,' the boy continued, 'we will all fly off to Holland or France and have a grand time there, before flying back for the morning. The fairies are entertained with many sorts of music besides my drum; they also have plenty of varieties of meats and wines!'

He said that these events usually took place on a Thursday and Burton asked him to return the following Thursday, to the same house. In the meantime, the captain made further enquires around Edinburgh and Leith and was assured by several people that nothing could keep the lad form meeting with his 'friends' on a Thursday. He was told people had tried to stop him before but none had succeeded.

So, when the boy turned up on the Thursday, it was to find Burton and half a dozen of his friends all tasked with keeping an eye on the boy. Again he was questioned, given money and some wine to drink, but as it approached eleven o'clock, he was suddenly gone from the room. Luckily, Burton managed to catch him as he reached the front door and brought him back to the room they had been in. However, a few minutes later, despite being under such close surveillance, the boy was gone again. This time he couldn't be found anywhere in the house.

Suddenly there were loud noises in the street outside. It seemed to be the boy shouting and Burton and his companions ran downstairs and out into the street. A large crowd had already gathered, perhaps drawn by the boy's shouting, but of the lad himself there was not a sight. He was gone. Search as hard as they could, both then and on several later occasions, neither Burton nor any of his friends ever saw the Fairy Boy of Leith again.

This story with the motif of fairy frolics inside notable hills is relatively common. Many such stories have musicians being lured in and kept for various lengths of time, and sometimes with truly tragic consequences but here the Fairy Boy is said to have been a regular, so – presumably – welcome visitor among the fairy folk. Of course Arthur's Seat, too, has its hidden cave, but it has Arthur and his men sleeping until the day of the land's greatest need calls them to rise again, to defend both the land and its people. Both these types of story point us back to ancient traditions regarding the ancestor peoples, who were perhaps themselves the actual origin of fairy beliefs in the first place. The idea of flying off abroad overnight for a bit of carousal is more associated with witches in Scottish tradition, but some of them undoubtedly were practitioners of behaviour that had links with long held beliefs, originating before the first Christian missionaries arrived in this part of the world. It may be that the Fairy Boy was a participant in an extant pre-Christian cult of some kind that held rituals on Calton Hill. The Australian poet Alexander Hope suggested in *A Midsummer Eve's Dream*, 1970, that such a fairy cult was extant in Edinburgh at the beginning of the sixteenth century. His book is a close analysis of Robert Dunbar's great Scots poem *The Tretis of the Tua Mariit Wemen and the Wedo*, and he explains the poem as essentially being about such a cult, echoing the reality that for a long time after the Protestant Reformation of 1560, people were continuing to perform what appear to be pre-Christian rites in many parts of Scotland. What this story underlines is that Calton Hill has different kinds of associations than just the scientific and practical associations that may be linked to very old ideas, indeed. And even in our modern world, there on the hill itself, with the drums of Beltane sounding as the fires send shadows flickering across the monuments around the hill, it is not at all hard to sense that the magic of this place has not entirely left it.

Declaration of Calton Hill

We, the People of Scotland demand our inalienable right to live within an accountable and democratic system of government and to determine the form that this system of government should take.

1. We demand a Parliament for Scotland, elected by and accountable to the People of Scotland. We further demand that the People of Scotland determine their relationship with the Government of the United Kingdom and, in the event of the people demanding independence, the relationships with other international bodies. A written constitutional agreement should be placed before the people for ratification.

2. All levels of government in Scotland should be elected by a fair voting system that responds to the people above all else.

3. Decisions should be taken at the lowest practical level, ensuring greater participation of the People of Scotland in the decision making process. Nobody should feel or be prevented from shaping and determining their environment, their society or their country.

4. Government, at all levels, should be open and information freely available. Individuals should have access to personal information pertaining to themselves.

5. Basic rights should be constitutionally enshrined, forming the foundations of freedom that all of Scotlands people should enjoy as of right.

We recognise that rule by consent of the people is at the heart of our nation's history and identity, and of all legitimate government. On April 9th 1992, three-quarters of Scottish voters supported parties advocating the establishment of a Scottish Parliament.

Sovereignty rests with the People of Scotland, and as such, we demand a referendum to determine the will of the People of Scotland.

We sign this Declaration of Calton Hill as a symbol of our commitment to work together to secure a democratic and accountable system of government in Scotland. We recognise that the legitimate demands of the People of Scotland to determine their political priorities will be best served by ending the futile barriers of conflict inherent in our present political system and by working together to deliver real democracy.

We sign this declaration 100 days after the result of the general election and 100 days after the start of the vigil outside Scotlands Parliament Building.

Let Scotland unite in a common cause — democracy for Scotland.

One of the most unusual artefacts to arise form the Vigil was the Declaration of Calton Hill. Composed communally in a series of meetings around the Vigil fire it was a statement of the aspirations of the Vigil folk and was printed up for the hundredth day of the Vigil, 18 July 1992. On that day a crowd gathered and the original copy of the Declaration was signed on the revere by a hundred people. These were people of all ages and walks of life, pulled together from all across Scotland by their common commitment to the simple idea of Democracy for Scotland.

Here it is in full:

The Declaration of Calton Hill

We the people of Scotland demand our inalienable right to live within an accountable and democratic system of government and to determine the form that this system of government should take.

1 We demand a Parliament for Scotland, elected by and accountable to the People of Scotland. We further demand that the People of Scotland determine their relationship with the Government of the United Kingdom and, in the event of the people demanding independence, the relationships with other international bodies. A written constitutional agreement should be placed before the people for ratification.

2 All levels of government in Scotland should be elected by a fair voting system that responds to the people above all else.

3 Decisions should be taken at the lowest practical level, ensuring greater participation of the People of Scotland in the decision making

process Nobody should feel or be prevented from shaping and determining their environment, their society or their country.

4 Government, at all levels, should be open and information freely available. Individuals should have access to personal information pertaining to themselves

5 Basic rights should be constitutionally enshrined, forming the foundations of freedom that all of Scotland's people should enjoy as of right.

We recognise that rule by the consent of the people is at the heart of our nation's history and identity, and of all legitimate government. On 9 April 1992, three-quarters of Scottish voters supported parties advocating the establishment of a Scottish Parliament.

Sovereignty rests with the People of Scotland, and as such, we demand a referendum, to determine the will of the People of Scotland.

We sign this Declaration of Calton Hill as a symbol of our commitment to work together to secure a democratic and accountable system of government in Scotland. We recognise that the legitimate demands of the People of Scotland to determine their political priorities will be best served by ending the futile barriers of conflict inherent in our present political system and by working together to deliver real democracy.

We sign this declaration 100 days after the result of the general election and 100 days after the start of the vigil outside Scotland's Parliament Building.

Let Scotland unite in a common cause – democracy for Scotland.

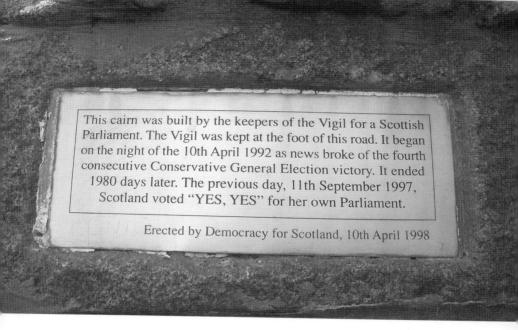

This cairn was built by the keepers of the Vigil for a Scottish Parliament. The Vigil was kept at the foot of this road. It began on the night of the 10th April 1992 as news broke of the fourth consecutive Conservative General Election victory. It ended 1980 days later. The previous day, 11th September 1997, Scotland voted "YES, YES" for her own Parliament.

Erected by Democracy for Scotland, 10th April 1998

Photographs on pages 2, 13, 16–17, 24–25, 29, 37, 40, 46, 48, 51, 59, 62–63, 66, 81, 91, 97, 110, 113, 121 and 122–123 courtesy of Stuart McHardy.

Photograph on page 74 courtesy of The Beltane Fire Society.

Share, explore, experience and celebrate our storytelling heritage.

0131 556 9579

The **Scottish Storytelling Centre** is the home of Scotland's stories on Edinburgh's picturesque Royal Mile. The Centre presents a seasonal programme of storytelling, theatre, dance, music and literature, supported by exciting visual arts, craft and multimedia exhibitions. The Centre also hosts the **Scottish International Storytelling Festival** in October, which is a highlight of Scotland's autumn.

You've seen the landscape, vibrant cities and historic buildings, now experience the magic of live stories and feed your imagination. Don't miss out on the warmth and energy of modern culture inspired by tradition!

www.scottishstorytellingcentre.co.uk

Some other books published by **LUATH** PRESS

Arthur's Seat: Journeys and Evocations

Stuart McHardy and Donald Smith
ISBN 978-1-908373-46-5 PBK £7.99

Arthur's Seat, rising high above the Edinburgh skyline, is the city's most awe-inspiring landmark. Although thousands climb to the summit every year, its history remains a mystery, shrouded in myth and legend.

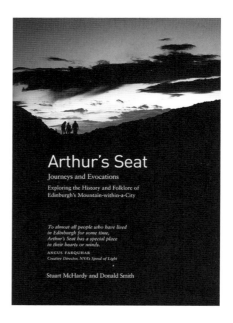

The first book of its kind, *Arthur's Seat: Journeys and Evocations* is a salute to the ancient tradition of storytelling, guiding the reader around Edinburgh's famous 'Resting Giant' with an exploration of the local folklore and customs associated with the mountain-within-a-city.

Inspired by NVA's Speed of Light, a major event in Edinburgh's International Festival and the country-wide Cultural Olympiad, *Journeys and Evocations* brings together past and future in a perspective of the Edinburgh landscape like no other.

Scotland the Brave Land: 10,000 Years of Scotland in Story

Stuart McHardy

ISBN 978-1-908373-46-6 PBK £7.99

In Scotland there is not a stream or a rock that does not have its story.
STUART McHARDY

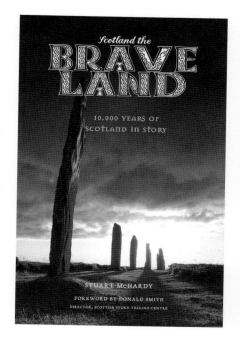

With the release of Disney-Pixar's *Brave*, the world's attention has been drawn to Scotland and its fascinating history. But *Brave* merely scrapes the surface of Scotland's rich storytelling culture. This collection of tales is the next step for anyone wishing to look further into the traditions of Scotland. These enchanting tales reflect the wide diversity of its heritage and there are few aspects of Scottish tradition that have escaped memorialisation in folklore.

With is captivation, and often gruesome, tales of heroic warriors in battle, bold heroines, deceitful aristocracy, and supernatural creatures, *Scotland the Brave* and is a journey into the cultural heritage and a glimpse at the folklore carried through oral tradition for more than 10,000 years.

Details of these and other books published by Luath Press can be found at:
www.luath.co.uk

Luath Press Limited

committed to publishing well written books worth reading

LUATH PRESS takes its name from Robert Burns, whose little collie Luath (*Gael.,* swift or nimble) tripped up Jean Armour at a wedding and gave him the chance to speak to the woman who was to be his wife and the abiding love of his life. Burns called one of 'The Twa Dogs' Luath after Cuchullin's hunting dog in Ossian's *Fingal*. Luath Press was established in 1981 in the heart of Burns country, and now resides a few steps up the road from Burns' first lodgings on Edinburgh's Royal Mile.
Luath offers you distinctive writing with a hint of unexpected pleasures.

Most bookshops in the UK, the US, Canada, Australia, New Zealand and parts of Europe either carry our books in stock or can order them for you. To order direct from us, please send a £sterling cheque, postal order, international money order or your credit card details (number, address of cardholder and expiry date) to us at the address below. Please add post and packing as follows: UK – £1.00 per delivery address; overseas surface mail – £2.50 per delivery address; overseas airmail – £3.50 for the first book to each delivery address, plus £1.00 for each additional book by airmail to the same address. If your order is a gift, we will happily enclose your card or message at no extra charge.

Luath Press Limited
543/2 Castlehill
The Royal Mile
Edinburgh EH1 2ND
Scotland
Telephone: 0131 225 4326 (24 hours)
Fax: 0131 225 4324
email: sales@luath.co.uk
Website: www.luath.co.uk